CULTURES OF THE WORLD
Cuba

Cavendish
Square
New York

Published in 2016 by Cavendish Square Publishing, LLC
243 5th Avenue, Suite 136, New York, NY 10016
Copyright © 2016 by Cavendish Square Publishing, LLC

Third Edition

This publication represents the opinions and views of the author based on his or her personal experience, knowledge, and research. The information in this book serves as a general guide only. The author and publisher have used their best efforts in preparing this book and disclaim liability rising directly or indirectly from the use and application of this book.
CPSIA Compliance Information: Batch #CW16CSQ
All websites were available and accurate when this book was sent to press.

Library of Congress Cataloging-in-Publication Data

Sheehan, Sean, 1951- author.
Cuba / Sean Sheehan, Leslie Jermyn, Debbie Nevins.
pages cm. — (Cultures of the world)
Includes bibliographical references and index.
ISBN 978-1-5026-0800-0 (hardcover) ISBN 978-1-5026-0801-7 (ebook)
1. Cuba—Juvenile literature. I. Jermyn, Leslie, author. II. Nevins, Debbie, author. III. Title.
F1758.5.S54 2016
972.91—dc23
2015031032

Writers, Sean Sheehan, Leslie Jermyn; Debbie Nevins, third edition
Editorial Director, third edition: David McNamara
Editor, third edition: Debbie Nevins
Art Director, third edition: Jeffrey Talbot
Designer, third edition: Jessica Nevins
Production Manager, third edition Jennifer Ryder-Talbot
Cover Picture Researcher: Stephanine Flecha
Picture Researcher, third edition: Jessica Nevins

PICTURE CREDITS

The photographs in this book are used with the permission of: Images Etc Ltd/Photolibrary/Getty Images, cover; lazyllama/Shutterstock.com, 1; Przemyslaw Skibinski/Shutterstock.com, 3; Tamara Kushch/Shutterstock.com, 5; Kamira/Shutterstock.com, 6; Regien Paassen/Shutterstock.com, 7; Kamira/Shutterstock.com, 8; The Visual Explorer/Shutterstock.com, 9; ffoto29/Shutterstock.com, 10; Planet Observer/Universal Images Group/Getty Images, 11; Evgenia Bolyukh/Shutterstock.com, 12; Lester Balajadia/Shutterstock.com, 13; Kamira/Shutterstock.com, 14; Laura Gooch/File:Priotelus temnurus -Camaguey, Camaguey Province, Cuba-8.jpg/Wikimedia Commons, 16; Angelo Giampiccolo/Shutterstock.com, 17; Kamira/Shutterstock.com, 18; Joseph Scherschel/The LIFE Picture Collection/Getty Images, 20; JCB Archive of Early American Images/File:DiegoVelazquezCuellar.jpg/Wikimedia Commons, 22; Michal Zalewski/File:Reconstruction of Taino village, Cuba.JPG/Wikimedia Commons, 23; Library of Congress/File:Havana 1639b.jpg/Wikimedia Commons, 24; Jorge G. Treche/File:Memorial José Martí, Cuba.jpg/Wikimedia Commons, 25; LC-DIG-det-4a25824/Library of Congress, 27; FPG/Hulton Archive/Getty Images, 28; Pictorial Parade/Getty Images, 29; Keystone-France\Gamma-Rapho via Getty Images, 30; Photo12/UIG via Getty Images, 32; Getty Image North America/Getty Image News/Getty Images, 34; Gregory Ewald/U.S. Coast Guard/Getty Images, 35; Chip Somodevilla/Getty Images, 36; MANDEL NGAN/AFP/Getty Images, 38; Dmitry Chulov/Shutterstock.com, 40; Philippe Antoine from Paris, France/ File:Todos a votar manana por la constitucion socialista.jpg/Wikimedia Commons, 42; Sven Creutzmann/Getty Images, 43; Marcel601/File:CDR-pinar-del-rio.jpg/Wikimedia Commons, 44; africa924/Shutterstock.com, 45; YAMIL LAGE/AFP/Getty Images, 46; PHB.cz (Richard Semik)/Shutterstock.com, 48; Vladimir Wrangel/Shutterstock.com, 50; Tupungato/Shutterstock.com, 53; nodff/Shutterstock.com, 54; danm12/Shutterstock.com, 55; Kamira/Shutterstock.com, 56; Sergey Uryadnikov/Shutterstock.com, 58; Alain Lauga/Shutterstock.com, 61; Imagezoo/Imagezoo/Getty Images, 62; Vlad61/Shutterstock.com, 63; lazyllama/Shutterstock.com, 64; Kamira/Shutterstock.com, 66; Kamira/Shutterstock.com, 68; © Angel Terry/Alamy, 69; Styve Reineck/Shutterstock.com, 70; Kamira/Shutterstock.com, 72; Konzept und Bild/ullstein bild via Getty Images, 73; Education Images/UIG via Getty Images, 75; Yavuz Arslan/ullstein bild via Getty Images, 76; villorejo/Shutterstock.com, 77; Roberto Machado Noa/LightRocket via Getty Images, 78; Noah Friedman-Rudovsky/Bloomberg via Getty Images, 79; Sarah L. Voisin/The Washington Post via Getty Images, 80; Sarah L. Voisin/The Washington Post via Getty Images, 82; L'Osservatore Romano Vatican-Pool/Getty Images, 83; Jan Sochor/LatinContent/Getty Images, 84; Konzept und Bild/ullstein bild via Getty Images, 85; Jan Sochor/age fotostock/Getty Images, 86; Sven Creutzmann/Mambo Photography/Getty Images, 87; Kamiraf/Shutterstock.com, 88; baldovina/Shutterstock.com, 89; Maridav/Shutterstock.com, 90; Aleksandar Todorovic/Shutterstock.com, 91; Marcin Krzyzak/Shutterstock.com, 93; Joe Raedle/Getty Images, 94; Merten Snijders/Lonely Planet Images/Getty Images, 95; Kamira/Shutterstock.com, 96; Roxana Gonzalez/Shutterstock.com, 97; Kamira/Shutterstock.com, 98; Areito/LatinContent/Getty Images, 99; David Redfern/Redferns/Getty Images, 100; tunart/E+/Gatty Images, 101; Ron Galella, Ltd./WireImage, 102; EMMANUEL DUNAND/AFP/Getty Images, 103; Ulf Andersen/Getty Images, 104;Kamira/Shutterstock.com, 106; Walter Bibikow/The Image Bank/Getty Images, 108; Ezra Shaw/Getty Images, 110; AP Photo/J. Pat Carter, 111; Ezra Shaw/Getty Images, 112; Joe Raedle/Getty Images, 114; The Visual Explorer/Shutterstock.com, 115; Kamira/Shutterstock.com, 116; Jan Sochor/Moment Editorial/Getty Images, 118; Fotosearch/Getty Images, 119; ALEJANDRO ERNESTO/AFP/Getty Images, 120; Christopher P. Baker/Lonely Planet Images/Getty Images, 122; YAMIL LAGE/AFP/Getty Images, 123; Bykofoto/Shutterstock.com, 124; Nico Tondini/Robert Harding World Imagery/Getty Images, 126; Gg/age fotostock/Getty Images, 127; Meißner/ullstein bild via Getty Images, 128; Lukas Hejtman/Shutterstock.com, 130; Windbreak/Shutterstock.com, 131; PromesaArtStudio/Shutterstock.com, 137.

PRECEDING PAGE

A row of brightly colored vintage American cars stand parked on a street in central Havana.

Printed in the United States of America

CONTENTS

CUBA TODAY

AH, CUBA. THE CARIBBEAN ISLAND EVOKES THE SULTRY, romantic aura of an old movie or an old memory—the warm, humid air; the sweet fragrance of tropical fruit; the sound of old men strumming guitars. In this movie, or memory, gentlemen smoke fat cigars and drive big, old-fashioned American cars down streets of pastel-colored buildings. Palm trees sway gently in the sea breeze while dark-haired women stroll by in light summer dresses. And everywhere, there is music.

For some people with long memories, this was Cuba. Havana, in particular, was an exotic hideaway for rich Americans, high-living high-rollers in a glittering tropical paradise of glamorous nightlife and lavish luxuries. For other people with long memories, the real Cuba was something else and somewhere else. It was in the countryside, where *macheteros*, or sugarcane cutters, barely made a living, and desperately poor peasants were hungry, malnourished, and illiterate.

Both of those Cubas are gone, though remnants remain. Cuba today still dances to the beat of a vivid and expressive culture. Lively Afro-Caribbean jazz fills the streets and the scent of cigar smoke lingers in the air. Havana retains much of its former

A typical Havana street scene includes people, old cars, and colorful buildings.

magnificence, from its pastel Spanish architecture to its soaring Baroque cathedrals to its grandiose El Capitolio, a near-replica of the Capitol building in Washington, DC. The casinos and high-rollers are gone, but old American cars still roll down the boulevards in pristine condition, as if fifty or sixty years haven't passed. (The US economic embargo prevents US automakers from selling their products in Cuba, so the Cubans just keep the old cars going and going.)

In reality, however, the city's splendor is rough around the edges. The elegant old buildings are crumbling. Their facades are weathered and decayed, and their formerly bright colors are faded and peeling. Murals of Che Guevara, the national hero, add an old-style radical flair to dilapidated walls. Nationalistic graffiti scrawls across condemned buildings, hailing Fidel Castro and the revolution. Many buildings are too dangerous to live in, which adds to the urban housing shortage.

In Cuba today, however, the government makes sure everyone has enough to eat, at least in principle. Everyone can read and even some taxi cab drivers are said to possess advanced university degrees. Health care is excellent, free, and available to all.

In short, Cuba today is a mix of innovation, progress, pride, stagnation, and disintegration. The communist revolution of 1958 swept out the extremes of capitalism—its wealthy elites and starving peasants—and improved many Cubans' lives, but the communist economy, hampered by its own internal flaws, its reliance on the former Soviet Union, and the US economic embargo, has not done well. In place of the former extremes, there is now a sort of broad, institutionalized poverty. This is largely the reason why thousands of Cubans continue to risk their lives each year by attempting to float across 90 miles (144.8 kilometers) of ocean to Florida.

Cubans are resourceful people. Lacking the wide range of market goods that Americans are accustomed to, they nevertheless have a healthy make-do attitude. For the most part, they support their revolution and have deep pride in their country and its rich cultural heritage. They are survivors, but they are not content with the status quo. They want a better life for themselves and their children.

These are interesting times for Cuba. Ever since the revolution, Cuba has been synonymous with the name Castro. Indeed, "Castro's Cuba" is such a common phrase that one would think the country belongs to one man. In a sense, it does, or did. In 2006, after more than fifty years in power, Fidel Castro stepped down as president for health reasons. His brother Raúl Castro assumed the office, which was not surprising. In 2013, however, Raúl announced that his second term in office would be his last—and that *was* surprising. Beginning in 2018, if all goes according to plan, the Castro regime in Cuba will come to an end.

Murals of the revolutionary hero Che Guevara are common throughout the country.

Tourists board a sightseeing bus in Havana.

What—and who—will come next? That question presents a tantalizing promise of change in this island nation where time seems to have stood still for half a century.

Coinciding with the end of the Castro era has been a change in US attitudes toward Cuba. By almost any measure, the hard-line US political approach that included diplomatic isolation and an economic embargo against Cuba simply did not work. The tough measures were intended to force Fidel Castro from office, but clearly they failed. US President Barack Obama pledged to take steps to normal relations with Cuba. In 2009, he eased some travel restrictions to the island. In December 2014, after a year and a half of secret negotiations, the two countries announced the restoration of diplomatic ties beginning in July 2015. In April 2015, Obama officially removed Cuba from the US State Department's list of state-sponsors of terrorism. That step alone removed a huge barrier to normalizing relations. As long as Cuba remained on that list, Cuba could not access most sources of international financing.

Both Cubans and Americans hailed these changes. In the United States, a 2015 poll found that 59 percent of Americans, including 56 percent of Latinos, approved of the recent US decision for diplomatic recognition of Cuba. These figures contrast greatly with those of just a few years before. However, people on both sides of the Florida Straits quickly realized that change will take time. That is, if the process of change continues at all.

There are massive barriers on both sides. The next US president could well take be a far less sympathetic view of Cuba. Furthermore, Cuban authorities are suspicious and reluctant to embrace too much change. The two biggest sticking points, the US embargo and the US naval base at Guantánamo Bay, both of which Cuba wants gone, will not be easily solved, if at all.

Even if barriers come down, there will be problems. Some people fear a mass invasion of US tourists will bring an overwhelming influx of American business, money, and influence. They grimly envision historic Old Havana

with a Starbucks and a McDonalds on every corner. As for the tourists themselves, one of their first problems could be a shortage of hotel rooms. Cuba's sixty thousand hotel rooms are already occupied near capacity by tourists from other countries, and many are not up to the standards that Americans usually expect.

Another concern is Cuba's cash-only economy for tourists. As of yet, Cuba does not have the capacity or the inclination to accept credit and bank cards. Perhaps that will soon change.

After Obama's December 2014 announcement, travel by Americans to Cuba jumped rapidly in January 2015. In fact, from October 2014 to through May 2015, visits to Cuba increased nearly 17 percent from the previous year, according to data from United States Customs and Border Protection. That number does not include the thousands more who got around the restrictions by entering Cuba through third countries, such as Canada and Mexico.

Clearly, there is a desire on the part of both countries to be good neighbors and put the past behind. If these changes do come to pass, they will surely affect Cuba, for better or for worse. Which will it be? The next few years will be interesting to watch. Bienvenido a Cuba!

Hotel Nacional (*at left*) is a Havana landmark.

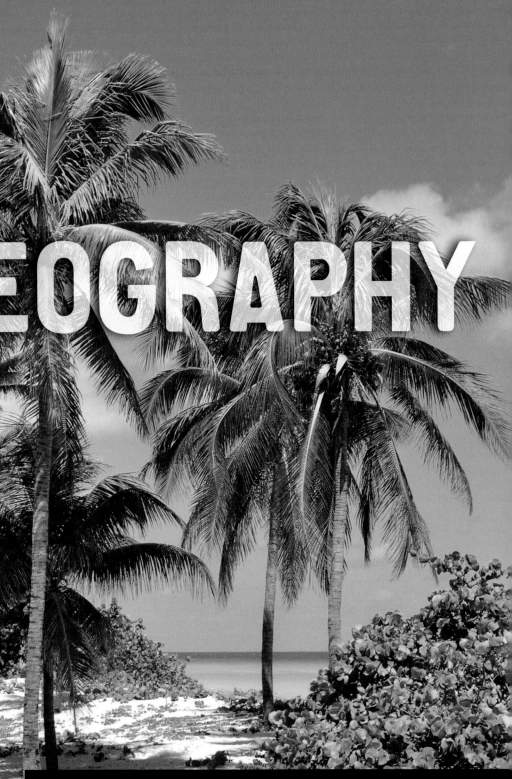

GEOGRAPHY

The resort town of Varadero, on Cuba's Hicacos Peninsula, offers tourists a 12-mile (20 km) stretch of luxurious sand and palms.

FOR MORE THAN FIFTY YEARS, THE distance between Cuba and the United States seemed immeasurably far. In fact, the average person found it nearly impossible to get from one place to the other. The distance was merely political, however.

Geographically, the countries are close neighbors. Cuba lies a mere 90 miles (144.8 km) off the southern coast of Florida. The distance between Cuba and the United States is close enough that some daredevils

This satellite view of Cuba shows its crocodile shape and close proximity to Florida. The smaller islands to the north of Cuba and southeast of Florida are the Bahamas.

1

Cuba is sometimes called *El Cocodrilo*, which means "crocodile" in Spanish. This is because, from the air, the island something like a crocodile or alligator.

have actually swum it. (Two, to be exact, and both were women.) Some people, desperate to leave Cuba, have floated from that nation to Florida on rafts or in small boats. Others have tried, but not survived. Before political relations between the two countries went sour around 1960, ferry boats used to routinely carry passengers from Miami to Havana—and back again. The largest of the Caribbean Islands, Cuba was a great tourist destination.

Cuba is the world's seventeenth-largest island. The islands are the visible summit of a submerged mountain range that once joined North America and South America. Cuba is 750 miles (1,207 km) long and ranges in width from 25 to 120 miles (40 to 193 km). It lies 90 miles (144.8 km) south of Florida and 90 miles (144.8 km) east of Mexico's Yucatán Peninsula. Cuba is slightly smaller than the state of Pennsylvania.

TOPOGRAPHY

The island of Cuba itself makes up nearly 95 percent of the national territory. The country also includes the *Isla de la Juventud*, or "Isle of Youth," off Cuba's southwestern coast as well as some 1,600 islets, most of them uninhabited.

An aerial view of the hills of Cuba

MOUNTAINS The island of Cuba consists mostly of flatlands and rolling plains, with mountains in the east and west and scattered across the long narrow island. The mountains make up almost a quarter of the total land mass.

The largest mountain range, the Sierra Maestra, is on the island's eastern point. It is 155 miles (249 km) long and contains Cuba's highest peak, *Pico Turquino* (6,476 feet; 1,974 meters). Another striking feature of the Sierra Maestra is *Gran Piedra* ("Huge Rock"), which is dominated by a sheer rock face that stretches to its summit at 3,936 feet (1,200 m). The central mountain range includes the Sierra de Trinidad. Here summits rarely exceed 4,000 feet

(1,220 m), so roads and railway lines have been built across these mountains, linking the southern shore with the northern coastline. The Sierra de los Órganos in the west is the lowest of the three main ranges, never exceeding 2,500 feet (762 m) and containing limestone caves.

CLIMATE

The climate in Cuba is temperate and semitropical. Trade winds that blow westward across the island produce a moderating influence on the weather. Cuba's dry season lasts from November to April and the wet season extends from May through October. The average minimum temperature is 73 degrees Fahrenheit (23 degrees Celsius) and the average maximum is 82°F (28°C). Temperatures occasionally exceed 100°F (38°C) in the summer, and during the winter, freezing temperatures are sometimes recorded in the high mountain areas.

Rainfall is generally moderate with three-quarters of the annual precipitation occurring during the wet season. The average annual rainfall is 52 inches (132 centimeters). While some years are characterized by drought, others receive very heavy rainfall. Both weather extremes have wreaked havoc in Cuba and on its peoples' lives.

A blustery day blows the palms' fronds.

Cuba lies in an area that experiences fierce tropical hurricanes. These storms typically form in tropical regions of the Atlantic Ocean and move westward, picking up power and speed as they go. Cuba is frequently in the path. On average, one hurricane every two years will hit Cuba, usually during the wet season. Hurricane season is July through November, with September and October being the months of highest hurricane probability.

Damage from hurricanes occurs from both wind and water. Heavy rains can dump 12 inches (30 cm) of rain in a period of twenty-four hours, but coastal areas are particularly vulnerable to storm surges. High winds cause ocean waters to rise up much higher than usual and flood the coast, especially at high tide.

In the last century, some historic hurricanes caused tremendous damage and loss of life on the island. The 1932 Cuba hurricane was the deadliest storm in Cuban history. (In those days, hurricanes weren't named the way they are today.) With sustained winds of 175 mph,

Hurricane waves hit the seawall in Havana.

(282 kph) the storm hit Cuba on November 9 and crossed the island in six hours, leaving 3,033 people dead.

Hurricane Flora in 1963 was a deadlier storm, though not for Cuba itself. Flora killed more than 1,750 in Cuba and 5,000 people in Haiti. In 2008, Hurricanes Gustav and Ike hit within two weeks of each other and caused tremendous damage. At least 200,000 Cubans lost their homes and the sugar crop was devastated. Today, Cuba is well equipped to forecast and better withstand a hurricane, though it can never be completely safe from these powerful storms.

WATERWAYS

Nearly six hundred rivers in Cuba, most of them short and not navigable, ensure that the land is well irrigated and suitable for agriculture. The two longest rivers are the Zaza, in central Cuba, and the Cauto, in eastern Cuba, north of the Sierra Maestra mountain range.

The largest and most interesting lake in Cuba is the *Laguna de la Leche* ("Milky Lagoon"), which is located near Cuba's northern coast. Since a number of channels connect the lagoon with the sea, tidal movements disturb the calcium carbonate deposits that form the floor of the lagoon and give rise to its milky appearance.

Crocodiles and alligators live along the coastal marshes and within the labyrinth of small rivers. There are large enclosed zones where thousands of these animals are farmed for their meat and their hides.

Cuba has many natural ports. The important ones include Cienfuegos, Havana, and Santiago de Cuba.

FAUNA

Cuba's isolation from other land masses has resulted in the development of unusually small species of fauna unique to Cuba. The banana frog, and the tiniest mammal in the world, the almiqui, are both found in Cuba. The nocturnal almiqui, or Cuban *Solenodon*, is an endangered shrew-like creature with long claws for catching insects. The smallest scorpion in the world can also be encountered in Cuba, which is less than a tenth of an inch long. Another minuscule creature is the *Polymita* genus of land snail, only found in the northeast of Cuba and believed by the early Afro-Cubans to have magical powers. None of the fourteen species of snakes inhabiting the island are poisonous, although one of them, the boa, kills by suffocating its prey by constriction and can grow to 13 feet (4 m) in length.

Nearly four hundred species of birds have been recorded on the island, including the bee hummingbird, the smallest in the world. Because it measures only 2 inches (5 cm), including the bill and tail, it is often confused

The primarily blue, red, and white Cuban trogon sports the same colors as the Cuban flag.

with an insect. One of the most eye-catching of the island's birds is the Cuban *Trogon*, a member of the Trogonidae family, which is made up of thirty-five species. These birds inhabit the tropical forests of the Americas, Africa, and Asia. The Cuban trogon is about the size of a small crow and its feathers are blue/metallic green with bright patches of black, red, and white. It enjoys special status as Cuba's national bird because it has the colors of the Cuban flag.

Butterflies and moths contribute to the kaleidoscope of color that characterizes the flora and fauna of Cuba. There are more than 180 species of butterflies, and of these nearly 30 are found only in Cuba. Their colorful displays can be imagined when they bear such names as Orange Sulphur, Mosaic, and Cuban Buff Zebra.

FLORA

Some 22 percent of Cuba's land is covered by forests and woods, so not surprisingly, there are a tremendous assortment of trees and flowers. Among the largest are the flame trees and the African tulip trees that provide shade during the heat of the day and advertise their presence with grand lily-like blooms. The frangipani, whose flowers are used for garlands, is common. Cuba's national flower is the butterfly jasmine, which has white flowers that look like butterflies. The climate encourages a colorful mixture of flowers to flourish. A typically eye-catching assortment around a home in the countryside may include pink or white congea climbing the walls and bougainvilleas of magenta, mauve, red, and orange crowding the path to the door.

The value of Cuban wood was appreciated by the Spanish, who used it to build their fleet of ships transporting treasure across the Atlantic. Today there is commercial value in the sale of mahogany, ebony, oak, and teak. The bark of mahogany is also used to treat ailments, including rheumatism and pneumonia. Cuba has more than sixty species of palm trees, including the stately royal palm, Cuba's national tree, which grows to over 75 feet (23 m)

LIFE IN THE WATER

With some nine hundred different species of fish in Cuban waters, it's not surprising that the island attracts tourists who like to fish. American writer Ernest Hemingway (1899–1961), who lived in Cuba for a number of years, was an enthusiast of big game fishing. The chance to catch a marlin, one of the fastest-swimming fish in the world, still draws tourists. There are various prestigious international fishing tournaments in Cuba, including the Hemingway Marlin Fishing Tournament begun by the writer in 1950.

The warm waters are home to a myriad collection of fish, including clown fish, queen angelfish, tangs, and blue striped grunts. On the surface, turtles swim placidly and share the water with dolphins and porpoises, while above them flying fish open their pectoral fins and scull the water with their tails to gain momentum. Underwater, the colorful fish life and impressive coral reefs can be appreciated with little more equipment than a pair of goggles. Certain areas of Cuban waters have been classified as biosphere reserves by UNESCO (United Nations Educational, Scientific and Cultural Organization).

Some of the fish found in Cuban waters are best appreciated from a safe distance. These include moray eels, which grow up to 5 feet (1.5 m) long and have sharp teeth that discourage divers from getting too close. Equally voracious predators are the barracudas (right), whose fang-like teeth have injured bathers and divers.

tall. The versatile tamarind tree, usually found lining roads, bears fruit pods used as a flavoring, preservative, and medicine, besides being a commercially valuable timber. Along the coastline grow almond, mangrove, and wild fig trees. Cuba's rarest tree is the cork palm, regarded as a living fossil because it has existed since the Cretaceous Period one hundred million years ago.

This view of Old Havana shows the Capitol building in the center of the skyline.

HAVANA

Three out of four people in Cuba live in the urban areas. The largest city is the capital, Havana, located in the northwest of the main island. It has a population of 2.1 million, or about 18 percent of the total Cuban population of 11.3 million.

In the sixteenth century, Havana became an important Spanish outpost in the Caribbean. For more than five hundred years the city has witnessed poverty and wealth and one rule after another. One of the most built-up areas in the capital, *Habana Vieja* ("Old Havana"), is the old colonial city. Situated on the shores of Havana Bay, Old Havana contains a number of buildings of outstanding architectural interest that date back to the period of Spanish colonization. In 1982, UNESCO listed Old Havana as a World Heritage city. Efforts are being made to restore many of these buildings. To accommodate the growing urban population, new housing has been built in the suburbs, creating small new townships.

OTHER CITIES

Cuba's second-largest city is Santiago de Cuba, which is on the southeastern end of the island, nestled in the foothills of the Sierra Maestra Mountains, overlooking a scenic bay. Around 427,000 people live there, many of whom are Cubans working at the US naval base at Guantánamo Bay less than 100 miles (161 km) away. Santiago de Cuba has an international airport and one of the country's busiest ports. There are numerous factories near the city, as well as an oil refinery and power stations. It is a very cosmopolitan city, due partly to the mix of African and Spanish heritages.

Santiago de Cuba, the country's first capital, is today known as the "Capital of the Revolution" because of its historical association with the overthrow of Fulgencio Batista's dictatorship. It was here in 1953 that a small group of rebels launched a surprise attack on the Moncada Barracks, an event regarded as a pivotal moment in Cuba's modern history.

Camagüey is a city in the center of Camagüey Province between Havana and Santiago de Cuba. This province is one of Cuba's most prosperous regions, mainly due to its agriculture and livestock.

INTERNET LINKS

www.cubanaturaleza.org/en
Cuba Naturaleza has photos and information in English about the geography and nature of Cuba.

www.eoearth.org/view/article/151558
The Encyclopedia of Earth chapter on Cuba has info on the island's ecology and biodiversity.

www.worldatlas.com/webimage/countrys/namerica/caribb/cuba/culand.htm
World Atlas has good maps and statistics.

HISTORY

The Argentinian-born Cuban revolutionary Ernesto Che Guevara (1928-1967), pictured here in 1959, is a revered figure in Cuba.

2

CUBA'S HISTORY HAS BEEN strongly influenced by its location. While that's true of most countries, it's especially true of Cuba. After all, Christopher Columbus landed here on his first excursion to the Americas. Even though he never quite knew where he was, the Spanish authorities figured it out quickly enough. Cuba became an important way station for ships sailing between the New World and Spain. Half a millennium later, Cuba's close proximity to the United States made its internal politics and foreign relations with communist countries particularly significant.

Throughout Cuba's history, a pattern of tensions between major players has been repeated: Spanish conquerors and settlers versus indigenous inhabitants; Spanish-born versus Cuban-born; landowners versus poor farmers; and more recently, the United States versus Cuba.

EARLY INHABITANTS

Cuba's earliest known inhabitants were the Ciboney and Guanahatabey, who lived in the western half of the island. Evidence of cave-dwelling peoples dates back to 3500 BCE. These include pictographs of magical signs.

The more numerous Taíno people arrived much later, around 1200 CE. They were closely related to the Arawaks of South America, and the two groups are often spoken of as one people. It is very likely that these early settlers on Cuba were descendants of people who had migrated north from the Amazon Basin of South America.

SPANISH RULE

In 1511, Diego Velázquez de Cuéllar arrived to establish a permanent settlement at Baracoa. The Spanish came to Cuba looking for gold. Taíno people panned the rivers and dug mines, and when more labor was needed, slaves from Africa were

An engraved portrait of Diego Velásquez de Cuéllar.

shipped to the island. When Cuba's yield of gold was found to be poor, the Spanish turned elsewhere. In 1519, a large expedition that included some three thousand Native people left Cuba under the command of Hernán Cortés. Lured by tales of riches, Cortés led his army to the Aztec Empire in Mexico. The African slaves were left on the island with the remaining Taíno people, to work on plantations in a system known as *encomienda* (ayn-koh-mee-AYN-da)—work in return for "protection" and conversion to Catholicism.

The remainder of the sixteenth century witnessed the decline and final elimination of the Taíno population. Black slaves became more important on plantations, although the development of Cuba's real wealth—sugar and tobacco—was slow. More and more Spanish ships stopped at Cuba in transatlantic crossings, laden with plunder from Mexico and Central and South America. The Spanish developed the harbor at Havana, and toward the end of the sixteenth century they built Morro Castle at the harbor entrance, signifying Cuba's newfound importance.

The Taíno lived in village communities varying in size from a few families to a few thousand people. Each community had a leader. They raised such crops as potatoes and manioc, grew yams and other vegetables, and caught fish and birds to eat. They wove cotton, cultivated the tobacco plant, and produced their own stone tools. Little is known about their religious beliefs, but idols were carved out of stone, wood, and clay.

The peaceful culture of the Taíno was ill suited to meet the challenge of Spanish invaders, who first landed on the island with Christopher Columbus on October 27, 1492. In later years, more Spanish arrived, and they had little trouble subduing the people, who they called Indians. The Taíno were forced into servitude. Those who resisted were killed. A missionary who accompanied the Spanish described how the Spanish "repaid" the hospitality of the Taíno by raping women and killing entire village populations. Children starved to death when parents were rounded up to work in mines.

A reconstruction of a Taino village in Cuba

The actual settlement of Cuba by Spain began in 1511. By then, other Caribbean islands had been settled. The leader of a community in Hispaniola, Chief Hatuey, fled to Cuba with his surviving followers. He tried to convince the Cuban Taíno to resist the invaders, but they mistrusted him. Hatuey went into hiding, joined by some Taíno, and when the Spanish arrived, he led his followers in guerrilla warfare against the Spanish. However, Taíno arrows were no match for horses and gunpowder, and their ambushes only delayed the inevitable. Hatuey was captured, and after he refused to reveal the location of his people, he burned at the stake. Within a very short time the Taíno faced extinction. They died fighting the invaders, from disease, from overwork in mines, and on plantations controlled by the Spanish.

The lettering in this painting reads: "Havana op't Eylant CVBA." The pen-and-ink and watercolor painting from about 1639 pictures Havana Harbor.

CUBA BECOMES IMPORTANT

It was well into the eighteenth century before the Spanish settlement in Cuba showed commercial success. Ships brought thousands of new slaves as sugar and tobacco became more profitable due to increased European demand and the opening of trade with the Spanish colonies and North America. Havana emerged as the obvious capital of the island as the harbor developed its own shipbuilding industry to complement its role as a major naval base.

As Havana became sufficiently important, it gained the attention of the British, who occupied the harbor and town in 1762. They stayed there for nearly a year before the Spanish regained control. By 1774 a census showed that the population had reached over 170,000, consisting of 44,000 blacks, 96,000 whites, and 31,000 people of mixed parentage.

During the decades that followed, the population swelled with thousands of French colonists, who fled neighboring Haiti seeking refuge from an uprising of Haitians. In 1801, Haiti invaded the eastern part of Hispaniola, and the Spanish colonists who had controlled part of the island also fled to Cuba. Two years later, when France sold Louisiana to the United States, more European colonials came to an increasingly prosperous Cuba. By the first decade of the nineteenth century, Cuba was economically self-sufficient and no longer depended on cash subsidies from Spain.

REVOLT AGAINST SPAIN

Long before slavery was abolished in Cuba in 1886, the population of Cuba was further mixed by the arrival of indentured Chinese laborers. The island's economy was booming, due chiefly to the sugar industry, and Cuba needed an alternative source of labor because of growing incidents of uprisings by black slaves. A focus of discontent at the time was the perception by Cuban-born Spanish known as *criollos* (kree-OH-yohs), or Creoles, that they were being discriminated against in favor of the *peninsulares* (pay-neen-soo-LAR-rays), or Spanish-born people living in Cuba. The government in Spain handed power and privileges to the peninsulares.

By the mid-nineteenth century, peninsulares and criollos clashed frequently in the pursuit of opposite aims. The peninsulares were mainly military personnel, government representatives, landowners, and slave-owners who preferred Spanish rule. The criollos included teachers, professionals, and writers, some of whom owned slaves. The criollos were divided, one group wanting independence from Spain but maintaining slavery, the other wanting freedom for everyone in Cuba.

Meanwhile, the United States was becoming increasingly interested in Cuba's economy and politics. Its offers to buy the island from Spain were officially rejected while attracting support within the business community on the island. Among the rebels watched closely by Cuba's powerful northern neighbor were Carlos Manuel de Céspedes, Antonio Maceo Grajales, and the best-loved and remembered of Cuban patriots, José Martí.

A memorial statue of José Martí in Havana.

"CUBA LIBRE!"

The first major revolt, known as the Ten Years' War (1868–1878), started with *El Grito de Yara* ("The Cry of Yara"). Yara was a town near the plantation of Carlos Manuel de Céspedes, a wealthy lawyer. He freed his slaves and proclaimed (the "cry") the independence of Cuba from Spain. Toward the end of the war, Spanish soldiers ambushed and shot Manuel.

The uneasy peace concluded in 1878 at the Convention of Zanjón did not solve the central issue of Cuba's status of independence. Spain was willing to liberalize its colonial rule, but calls for independence or incorporation into the United States were not answered. The inconclusive Ten Years' War left approximately 50,000 Cubans and 208,000 Spanish dead.

Antonio Maceo, known to Cubans as the Bronze Titan, joined the rebels and contributed greatly to their guerrilla tactics. When not ambushing the Spanish, he read widely and organized the rebels' living quarters, including hospitals and food stores, with the help of his mother and wife. After the Ten Years' War, he left for Jamaica with his family and continued the revolutionary struggle from abroad. There he met José Martí, whom many called the Apostle of Freedom.

A war of independence erupted again in 1895, with both sides showing a grim determination to resolve the conflict through violence. The rebels were led by Martí, whose rallying call was *"Cuba Libre."* Within three years Spain controlled only the coastal towns.

Martí was convinced of the need for Cuba to develop as an independent country. When he was only sixteen, he was sentenced to hard labor in a stone quarry, imprisoned on the Isle of Pines (later known as *Isla de la Juventud*, or Isle of Youth), then banished to Spain because of his political opinions. In Spain he graduated with a law degree in 1874, and his revolutionary fervor expressed itself in poetry and prose. Banned from Cuba, Martí traveled to the United States where he campaigned relentlessly for an independent Cuba. He established the Cuban Revolutionary Party in New York and sought to enlist the aid of the US government, but it was not prepared to help him officially. In 1895 he organized an armed force that landed in Cuba. Thousands of Cubans died in the rebellion that followed, including Martí, who was killed during an encounter with troops loyal to the Spanish government. The best-loved leader of the Cuban revolution died when he was only forty-two. Many statues have been erected in his memory. Generally less well-known is the fact that he wrote the verses of the famous song "Guantanamera" ("A Girl from Guantanamo") and that he was the grandfather of actor César Romero, who played The Joker in the 1960s *Batman* television series.

US RULE

At first, the United States remained officially neutral during the tumultuous events in Cuba, though secretly it was negotiating with Spain to purchase the island. US business companies, by then the dominant investors in Cuba's sugar industry, called for US intervention in Cuba to protect their interests. Then in February 1898, an event occurred that caused the United States to enter the war to free Cuba from Spain.

The battleship USS *Maine* was sent to Havana with the ostensible mission of helping to evacuate US citizens endangered by the fighting between Cuban revolutionaries and loyalist forces. When the ship exploded in the harbor in February 1898, under circumstances that have never been fully explained, the United States blamed Spain and declared war on the country. This was the start of the Spanish-American War, which was one-sided and brief because Spain was unprepared for military engagement in its colony.

The sinking of the USS *Maine* was a catalyst to war between the United States and Spain. However, the explosion might have been caused by an onboard fire that ignited the ship's armaments.

With US troops as well as nationalist rebels fighting against the loyalist troops, the war came to an end in August 1898. In December 1898, under the Treaty of Paris, Spain relinquished its claim to the island. A US military government was set up to govern the island.

For three years following the Treaty of Paris, US army general Leonard Wood governed Cuba. The army mainly worked on public works programs, such as the building of schools and roads, in order to facilitate US economic and cultural development of Cuba.

Although the United States brought order to the war-torn island, many Cubans believed they had exchanged one undesirable master for another. There was also a sense of bitterness that, through one single incident, the revolutionaries had been denied the glory of winning a war that had lasted decades and cost so many Cuban lives.

CONTINUED US INFLUENCE

To satisfy Cuban nationalism, the US administration helped draw up a new constitution in 1901 that granted Cuba a degree of self-rule in 1902, but Afro-Cubans were denied the vote, and the Platt Amendment, which the

Cuban military and political leader Fulgencio Batista (1901–1973) drives through the streets of Havana in March 1952, greeting his loyal fans. He was president of Cuba from 1940 to 1944 and from 1952 to 1959. The slogan on the car reads "Batista—He's the Man."

United States insisted had to be part of the constitution, established the right of the United States to intervene in the island's affairs. The amendment also gave the United States the right to buy or lease land for naval bases. Accordingly, in 1903, a permanent lease on Guantánamo Bay was granted to the United States. The naval base is still in operation today.

From 1906 to 1910 US troops returned to the island because of frequent uprisings against government leaders who were more interested in accumulating power and personal wealth than in the people's welfare. During the 1920s, a dramatic rise in the price of sugar brought prosperity, but because US companies owned most of the profitable concerns, many Cubans were denied the fruits of economic success.

When the Great Depression in the 1930s worsened the already bad conditions, the regime of President Gerardo Machado was seriously threatened. In 1933, an army sergeant, Fulgencio Batista, organized a coup against Machado. Batista had US support and became Cuba's next leader.

BATISTA'S DICTATORSHIP

Fulgencio Batista (1901—1973) ruled as commander in chief of the armed forces from 1934 to 1939. He was elected president in 1940. He governed Cuba well and made improvements to the infrastructure.

The constitution allowed a president to serve only one four-year term in office. In 1952, however, Batista staged a second coup and ruled as Cuba's dictator before being deposed himself in 1959. Commerce became brisk because of the government's repression of trade unions. Foreign companies set up businesses in Cuba and exported their profits. This time, Batista apportioned little money for public works, as large-scale corruption permeated every aspect of political life. Havana became the playground of the wealthy with its profusion of casinos, bars, and brothels. The tourists who filled Havana's casinos were oblivious to the poverty underpinning the private wealth of a minority of politicians and their close supporters. In the rural areas especially, many families could barely feed themselves, and it was common to see malnourished children.

CASTRO'S REVOLUTION

The young lawyer Fidel Castro (b. 1926) had planned to contest the 1952 elections, but when these never took place he adopted more direct action. On July 26, 1953, he led a small group, which included his brother Raúl, in an attack on the Moncada Army Barracks in Santiago de Cuba. The rebellion failed, and Castro was imprisoned.

Cuban President Fidel Castro speaks in New York City during a visit to the United States in 1959.

After his release in 1955, Castro went to Mexico to plan a second attempt at overthrowing the Batista dictatorship. A close colleague at this stage was the famous Argentinean revolutionary, Che Guevara. In December 1956, Castro, Guevara, and about eighty others landed in eastern Cuba. Most of the group were killed or captured, but twelve men, including Castro and Guevara, hid in the mountains of the Sierra Maestra.

Over the next two years they conducted an increasingly successful guerrilla campaign against the government. The initial group of twelve was joined by supporters who shared their vision of freedom. The rebels gained the support of ordinary Cubans.

Elections were organized for November 3, 1958. Batista's chosen supporter was elected president, but it meant little. Soon after, the army deserted Batista, who fled Cuba on January 1, 1959. The rebel army marched into Havana on January 8, and a new era in Cuba's history began.

FRICTION WITH THE UNITED STATES

The downfall of Batista's repressive government was hailed as a triumphant victory both in Cuba and around the world. The corruption and inequality that characterized Batista's Cuba had long been known. Over the next

Fidel Castro was born in 1926, the son of a sugar plantation owner from Spain. He was an exceptional athlete in high school. In 1945, he entered the University of Havana, where he received a PhD in law in 1950.

After graduating, he joined the Cuban People's Party, named Partido Ortodoxo. *He began working toward the goal of revolution in Cuba. By 1958, he realized that goal and emerged as the revolutionary leader of Cuba. He would become the longest-serving national leader in the world. Contrary to expectations, he did not become a typical tin-pot dictator. Unlike many dictators, Castro did not actively seek to install a cult of personality in Cuba. He did not erect statues of himself all over the country. Nevertheless, Cuba was*

so completely dominated by this one man for so long that a sort of de facto cult of personality arose anyway.

Castro, shown here in 1968, keeps his personal life very private. Most Cubans know little about his family and have hardly seen pictures of his family members in the media—except, of course, for his brother Raúl. Fidel is known to have seven, possibly nine, sons and two daughters, by various women.

Over the years, Castro survived numerous attempts on his life, some of them arranged by the US Central Intelligence Agency (CIA). His ability to talk at length is legendary. During the 1960s and 1970s, it was common for him to deliver a speech of three or four hours. In 1969 he spoke on television for seven hours non-stop!

couple of years, however, relations between Cuba and the United States deteriorated. By January 1961 diplomatic relations between the two countries were formally broken.

The rupture was caused by Castro's determination to build a revolutionary new society based on socialism. Cuba lowered rents by half and put industries under state control. The principal losers were US companies or individuals who owned these enterprises and buildings. The Cuban government took over US-owned sugar estates and cattle ranches, and then seized the oil refineries. The government confiscated about $1 billion in US-owned properties. In response, the US government imposed a trade embargo against Cuba in October 1960. Cuba then seized all remaining US assets.

Cuban refugees poured into the United States after the downfall of the Batista government. They included officials of the Batista government, those involved in corruption and vice, and ordinary Cuban citizens opposed to Castro. Many of the exiles formed an underground movement to plan the invasion of Cuba. In late 1959, some exiles launched sporadic firebomb attacks. Though not officially sanctioned by the United States, these attacks used US planes and ammunition. The attacks increased tension between the two countries.

In February 1960, Cuba and the Soviet Union signed their first trade agreement. As Russian trade and assistance grew, the US government became increasingly concerned by Castro's leftist leanings. In 1961, the United States supported an attempt by Cuban exiles opposed to Castro to invade the island at the Bay of Pigs. The invasion was a disaster.

CASTRO'S POLICIES

As the country's leader, Castro was devoted to the ideals of socialism. He believed that capitalism, the economic system of the United States and many other Western nations, inevitably created an unfair class structure in society—one in which one class of people lived much better lives than did those in a lower class. Castro believed the upper class got rich and remained rich by profiting from the low-paid labor of the lower classes. He therefore

"The ever more sophisticated weapons piling up in the arsenals of the wealthiest and the mightiest can kill the illiterate, the ill, the poor, and the hungry, but they cannot kill ignorance, illness, poverty, or hunger." —Fidel Castro, 2002, in a speech in Monterrey, Mexico

Operation Pluto was the secret name of an invasion planned by the exiles with help from the US CIA. Its aim was to train 1,500 Cuban exiles, arm them, and help them land on Cuba, where Cubans were expected to welcome their liberators.

It started with the bombing of two Cuban airfields on April 15, 1961, which killed seven and wounded forty-four. The US planes used were marked with the Cuban military insignia, to give the illusion of a military uprising. Rumors of the landing alerted the Cuban authorities, who rounded up anti-government suspects, including foreign journalists and CIA agents.

The invasion force landed on April 17 in the Bay of Pigs at Playa Giron. Within forty-eight hours, the invaders were captured. The incident increased Castro's popularity, especially since he was seen in action, organizing troops at Playa Giron. About 120 men were killed in the confrontation, and nearly 1,200 captured. The leaders were returned to the United States in exchange for cash, and the rest in exchange for medicine and food.

Mercenaries were captured and held as prisoners after landing at the Bay of Pigs in 1961.

considered capitalism to be an evil system and he intended to do away with it in Cuba. He did that by nationalizing all private industry.

Castro also wanted all Cubans to have sufficient food, health care, housing, and education. He achieved some of those goals, especially in education and health care. Under his rule, Cuba greatly increased life expectancy, lowered infant and child mortality rates, eliminated illiteracy, and improved education for all. The Cuban health care system became one of the best in Latin America, and provided universal health care. In the 1990s, Cuba had an abundance of doctors and nurses, and sent many of the professionals overseas on humanitarian missions to needy countries.

However, Castro's successes came at a price—and that price was human rights and individual freedoms. Castro's regime was extremely repressive and allowed for no political dissent. Anyone who opposed his vision of a socialist, nationalist Cuba was considered a counter-revolutionary and jailed. Castro defended this policy, stating that the state must limit the freedoms of individuals and imprison those involved in counter-revolutionary activities in order to protect the rights of the collective populace.

COMING TO AMERICA

One of the rights that Cubans did not enjoy under Fidel Castro was the ability to leave the country. (A policy of not allowing ordinary citizens to leave the homeland is common under the rule of a dictatorship.)

RAFTERS Every year, an estimated three thousand Cubans attempted to flee to Florida—some years, many more. Desperate people tried to sail or float across the Strait of Florida, the 90-mile-plus (150 km) stretch of sea that separates Cuba and Florida. Often they came in overcrowded, small open boats or rickety rafts they had secretly assembled by hand. Some never made it at all, drowning when their unsafe crafts sank or capsized. For those who did make it, the United States put out the welcome mat.

MARIEL BOATLIFT In 1980, Castro announced that anyone wanting to leave Cuba could do so. He provided boats out of the port of Mariel for this purpose. Within weeks, a mass exodus of 125,000 Cuban refugees arrived in Southern Florida, overwhelming US officials. The Mariel boatlift, as it came to be called, was at first cheered in the United States. However, the arrival of hoards of homeless, jobless people quickly turned American sentiment. The situation caused a political problem for President Jimmy Carter, especially after it was revealed that Castro had included 2,746 criminals, mentally ill patients, and other "undesirables" among the refugees.

"There is often talk of human rights, but it is also necessary to talk of the rights of humanity. Why should some people walk barefoot so that others can travel in luxurious cars? . . . Why should some be miserably poor so that others can be hugely rich? I speak on behalf of the children in the world who do not have a piece of bread. I speak on the behalf of the sick who have no medicine, of those whose rights to life and human dignity have been denied."
—Fidel Castro

In 1962, the world came perilously close to a nuclear war. As Cuba became more isolated by the hostility of the United States, it increasingly turned to the Soviet Union for support. The Soviet Union responded to Cuba's request for military assistance to reduce the risk of another US-backed invasion like the Bay of Pigs incident.

In the summer of 1962, US spy planes gathered photographic evidence of Soviet missile installations in Cuba. The United States felt threatened because the missiles had a range of 1,000 miles (1,609 km), and Soviet jet bombers, also in Cuba, were capable of carrying nuclear weapons. On October 22, 1962, President John F. Kennedy warned his country of the threat from a nuclear attack and demanded that the Soviet Union dismantle the sites. He made it clear that not dismantling the missile sites would be viewed as a hostile act justifying nuclear retaliation by the United States.

The United States put a naval blockade around Cuba to halt further shipments of arms. On October 28, 1962, Soviet premier Nikita Khrushchev confirmed the missiles would be removed from Cuba if the United States promised not to invade the island. The offer was accepted and war was averted.

The Cuban missile crisis was seen as a confrontation between two world powers. Fidel Castro was angry that he was not consulted before Khrushchev's decision, which he disagreed with, but he did not have the power to act.

A P2V Neptune US patrol plane flies over a Soviet freighter during the Cuban missile crisis in this 1962 photograph.

WET FOOT, DRY FOOT In an effort to prevent a repeat of that calamity, and to discourage rafters, the US adopted a new policy toward Cuban refugees. In 1995, the United States adopted a policy of "wet foot, dry foot" toward the rafters. If a migrant made it to dry US land ("dry foot"), he or she could request legal permanent resident status and possible eventual US citizenship. If, on the other hand, the migrant was intercepted at sea ("wet foot"), he or she was almost always turned away. The US Coast Guard worked hard to prevent any Cubans from making it to dry land. It actively watched for rafters.

Although the intercepted Cubans could apply for asylum on the claim of facing political persecution at home, it was very difficult to achieve. Nevertheless, those who were sent back to Cuba faced a particularly difficult time for having tried to escape. Despite a great deal of criticism of the "wet foot, dry foot" policy, it remained in effect as of 2015. However, the 2015 agreement to resume normal diplomatic Cuban—US relations gave rise to anticipation in both countries that the policy would soon be changed.

Cuban migrants try to reach the Florida coast on board a makeshift boat made out of a 1951 Chevrolet truck with a propeller driven off the drive shaft on July 16, 2003. The US Coast Guard intercepted the rafters and returned the twelve migrants to Cuba.

The most notorious US prison sits on Cuban land, and the Cubans are not happy about it. The Guantanamo Bay Detention Camp is a US military prison located within Guantanamo Bay Naval Base on the eastern shore of Cuba. The naval base, also called GTMO (pronounced "gitmo") by military personnel, takes up 45 square miles (120 square kilometers) of land and water at Guantánamo Bay. The United States leases the property in accordance with provisions of the Cuban-American Treaty of 1903.

The United States built a naval base there, the oldest overseas US naval base, and in 2002 built the military prison. It was specifically built to house combatants captured in the Afghanistan and Iraq wars. It also holds prisoners related to the War on Terror, the US military response to the September 11, 2001 terrorist attacks in New York and Washington, DC.

The detention camp has proven to be a particular source of controversy, raising international—not just Cuban—objections. The administration of President

Outside the White House in Washington, DC, in May 2014, demonstrators demand the closing of the military prison at Guantanamo Bay, Cuba.

George W. Bush, which built the prison, insisted that the prisoners had no right to the protection of the Geneva Conventions. The prisoners were deemed to be unlawful combatants; that is, they were not soldiers representing any recognized nation, and therefore not covered by the treaties governing prisoners of war. Alleged acts of torture and inhumane treatment have been reported. Since January 2002, 779 men have been brought to Guantanamo; as of January 2015, 122 detainees remained.

Although President Barack Obama campaigned on the promise to close the prison, Congressional objection has so far (as of 2015) prevented it. The prison controversy only exacerbates the already difficult relations between Cuba and the United States.

Cuba regards the US presence in Guantánamo Bay as illegal. It insists the Cuban–American Treaty was obtained by threat of force and is in violation of international law. Although the United States pays Cuba $4,085 a year for the lease of the land—a figure that dates to1934—Cuba has never cashed the checks.

COLD WAR

During the height of the Cold War between the United States and the Soviet Union, Cuba openly supported a variety of socialist regimes. Cubans fought in Angola, Ethiopia, and Nicaragua. This deepened US hostility toward Castro. After the collapse of the Soviet Union in 1991, Cuba no longer had the capacity to arm or fight for other regimes, but the US government continued to tighten the trade embargo in order to loosen Castro's hold on power.

In 1996, the United States enacted the Cuban Liberty and Democratic Solidarity Act, also known as the Helms-Burton Act. This law prohibited any foreign company that did business in the United States from trading with or in Cuba. The act was widely resisted by the European Union, Canada, and Mexico. In the following years, the law was amended and loosened somewhat.

In 2004 US President George W. Bush restricted cash remittances from Cubans in the United States to their relatives in Cuba. Castro retaliated by revoking the 1993 law that permitted Cubans to hold US dollars and imposed a 10 percent surcharge on dollar conversions to Cuban pesos.

Cuba was not viewed by most of the world as a rogue state or a threat. The US sanctions, while inconvenient for Cubans and Cuban-Americans, did

US President Barack Obama (*right*) shakes hands with Cuba's President Raúl Castro during a meeting at the Summit of the Americas on April 11, 2015 in Panama City.

not have enough international support to damage Castro. Indeed, some argue that they bolstered his popularity by strengthening Cuban nationalism.

FIDEL STEPS DOWN

In 2006, as Castro's health began to falter, he delegated his presidential responsibilities to his brother, Vice President Raúl Castro. In 2008, the National Assembly of People's Power unanimously chose Raúl to be Cuba's new president. Nevertheless, Raúl continued to consult with Fidel on governmental matters. In 2011, Fidel resigned his post as leader of the Communist Party. Again, Raúl took his place.

A THAW IN RELATIONS

In December 2014, President Obama and President Raúl Castro announced that the United States and Cuba would restore full diplomatic ties for the first time in more than fifty years. The agreement came after eighteen months of secret talks between US and Cuban officials. The negotiations were encouraged and brokered by Pope Francis.

In April 2015, Obama and Raúl Castro met at the Summit of the Americas Conference in Panama City, Panama. It was the first meeting between a US and Cuban head of state since the two countries severed their ties in 1961. The first thing they agreed to do was to reopen embassies in Havana and Washington, DC.

INTERNET LINKS

immigration.about.com/od/immigrationlawandpolicy/a/U-S-Allows-Cuban-Migrants-Different-Treatment.htm
About News explains the wet foot, dry foot immigration policy.

www.bbc.com/news/world-latin-america-19576144
The BBC has a timeline of Cuban history beginning in 1492.

www.cfr.org/cuba/us-cuba-relations/p11113
The Council on Foreign Relations explains the history of US—Cuban relations.

www.cnic.navy.mil/regions/cnrse/installations/ns_guantanamo_bay.html
This is the official website of the US Naval Station Guantanamo Bay.

www.mapsofworld.com/infographics/poll/will-guantanamo-bay-ever-be-shut-down-facts-infographic-text.html
This page includes an in-depth infographic charting the situation at the Guantanamo Detention Camp.

topics.nytimes.com/top/news/internationalcountriesand territories/cuba/index.html
The *New York Times* Topics section provides up-to-date news articles about Cuba.

GOVERNMENT

Cuba's Capitol Building gleams in the October sun in Havana.

3

I N 2018, IF ALL GOES ACCORDING TO plan, Cuba will be led by someone other than a Castro for the first time in more than fifty-four years. Fidel Castro stepped down in 2008 and passed the presidency to his brother Raúl Castro. In 2013, Raúl announced that he would retire at the end of his term in 2018. In 2013, Raúl selected Miguel Diaz-Canel (b. 1960) to serve as the country's vice president, and as such, he is expected to become the next president of Cuba.

The Cuban presidency is not an elected position. Cuba's system of government is defined in its constitution as "a socialist state of workers and peasants, and all other manual and intellectual workers." Political power is exercised through the Cuban Communist Party, and Cuba is one of the few countries in the world still committed to the revolutionary ideologies of Karl Marx and Vladimir Ilyich Lenin.

CONSTITUTION

The Cuban Constitution now in effect was written in 1976, and has been amended three times, most recently in 2002. It affirms socialism as the irrevocable form of government. It establishes that the president is the

The opening lines of the Cuban Constitution read, in part, as follows:

WE, CUBAN CITIZENS,

heirs and continuators of the creative work and the traditions of combativity, firmness, heroism and sacrifice fostered by our ancestors:

by the Indians who preferred extermination to submission;

by the slaves who rebelled against their masters;

by those who awoke the national consciousness and the ardent Cuban desire for an independent homeland and liberty;

by the patriots who in 1868 launched the wars of independence against Spanish colonialism and those who in the last drive of 1895 brought them to the victory of 1898, victory usurped by the military intervention and occupation of Yankee imperialism;

by the workers, peasants, students, and intellectuals who struggled for over fifty years against imperialist domination, political corruption, the absence of people's rights and liberties, unemployment and exploitation by capitalists and landowners; ...

A poster urges voters to vote for the socialist constitution.

GUIDED

by the ideology of José Martí, and the sociopolitical ideas of Marx, Engels, and Lenin; ...

AWARE

that all the regimes of the exploitation of man by man cause the humiliation of the exploited and the degradation of the human nature of the exploiters;

that only under socialism and communism, when man has been freed from all forms of exploitation—slavery, servitude and capitalism—can full dignity of the human being be attained; and that our Revolution uplifted the dignity of the country and of Cubans ...

head of state, leader of the government, and the commander of the armed forces. The Council of State issues laws in the form of decrees and is made up of the president, six vice presidents, a secretary, and twenty-three other members. The Council of Ministers—the president, vice presidents, and ministers—is the chief administrative organ with executive power.

THE NATIONAL ASSEMBLY

The 609-member National Assembly of People's Power is elected directly by universal suffrage. Candidates are nominated at meetings with a number of work organizations, including the armed forces and student groups. The election for the National Assembly held in 1993 was the first election in which citizens went to the polls and voted in secret.

Voting is non-compulsory and is a right of Cuban citizens who have resided on the island for at least two years. Voting age is sixteen. Convicted criminals and the mentally handicapped are not allowed to vote. Cubans living abroad are also denied the right to vote.

President Raúl Castro delivers a speech to the National Assembly in December 2014.

A political sign in Pinar del Río, Cuba

Seventy-five percent of the members of the National Assembly are Communist Party members. There are no legal opposition parties so candidates either run as Communists or as independents. All elected government officials, including members of the National Assembly, are elected to five-year terms. Efforts by dissidents to have Cubans protest by spoiling their ballots have been largely unsuccessful.

The members of the Supreme Court, Council of State, and Council of Ministers, including the president, are chosen by the National Assembly. The National Assembly also selects members of the judicial arm of the government.

THE COMMUNIST PARTY

The 1976 constitution guarantees that the Communist Party shall remain the only legitimate party in Cuba. The Constitution states that the party is the "leading force of society and of the state" and as such has the capability of setting national policy.

The structure of the party is similar to that of the government. There is a Central Committee of 150 deputies elected at party congresses. Deputies elect members of the Politburo who form a ruling body. A party congress is held approximately every five years. The first was held in Havana in 1975. These are opportunities for delegates of the party from all over the island to convene to discuss reforms and future plans.

LOCAL GOVERNMENT

The country is divided into fifteen provinces that form the basis for the administrative and political organs of power. From east to west, they are Guantánamo, Santiago de Cuba, Holguín, Granma, Las Tunas, Camagüey, Ciego de Avila, Sancti Spiritus, Villa Clara, Cienfuegos, Matanzas, Mayabeque,

Is Cuba a democracy? The answer depends on one's definition of democracy, which means "rule by the people." In the United States, the Cuban model certainly defies the basic concepts of individual freedom that are the foundation for a liberal democracy. Cuba, however, considers itself a "people's democracy," which is defined in a different way. The phrase first emerged as a Marxist-Leninist concept, developed after World War II. It describes a society in transition from liberal democracy to socialism. However, Cuba's form of government can no longer be considered "in transition" to socialism.

Cuba's form of democracy is also sometimes called a revolutionary democracy. However, certain international human rights organizations reject the notion that Cuba is democratic in any sense. Here are some of the characteristics of each form of government:

LIBERAL DEMOCRACY *The essential elements of this form of government include*
- *the protection of individual rights—human rights, civil rights, civil liberties, and political freedoms;*
- *fair, free, and competitive elections between multiple distinct political parties;*
- *separation of governmental powers and a system of checks and balances between them; and*
- *representational or direct participation in government.*

PEOPLE'S DEMOCRACY *This form of government*
- *is usually the result of a revolutionary movement which has seized power in the name of the people;*
- *is one in which individual rights are superseded by the will of the people as a whole;*
- *gives citizens a choice of electoral candidates only at the lowest, or municipal, levels; and*
- *has a one-party system.*

A Cuban man rides his bicycle past graffiti hailing Fidel Castro, on August 12, 2014, in Havana.

La Habana, Artemisa, and Pinar del Río. There are 169 municipalities; one, the Isle of Youth, is a special division.

Local government is based around provincial and municipal assemblies. Members of municipal assemblies are elected to terms of two-and-a-half years, and each municipal assembly is headed by an executive committee. Members of these executive committees form the provincial assemblies.

Another important organization of local administration is known as the Committee for the Defense of the Revolution. The neighborhood bodies that form this organization are the most local form of government. The name of the organization goes back to the early days of the revolution when an invasion from the United States was a very real threat and surveillance groups were established to counter it.

POLULAR SUPPORT FOR THE GOVERNMENT

For the most part, Cubans support their government. The system has provided them a standard of health, education, and cultural enrichment that is superior to the majority of Latin American and Caribbean countries. The government has reduced the gap between rich and poor so that when there are hard times, everyone suffers together. It is not a perfectly equal society but everyone is educated, has access to medical care, and has his or her basic needs guaranteed.

On the minus side, the Castro government does not tolerate political opposition. Underground groups of dissidents exist and are subject to sudden arrest and imprisonment. Under Cuban law, dissidents can be jailed for "social dangerousness," which does not require them to commit any specific offense. Instead, a suspected "proclivity to commit a crime," such as showing "contempt to the figure of Fidel Castro," can lead to jail. According to the organization Reporters Without Borders, the Cuban media is among the least free in the world. Past attempts by the United States to destabilize Cuba gives the government a reason for feeling paranoid and an excuse for harassing those who are committed to peaceful political change.

There is a tension in Cuba between those who remember life under Batista and US influence and the younger generations who only know the difficulties of living in Cuba. Older people tend to support the revolution and Castro because they fear a return to grinding poverty, inequality, and ignorance. Younger Cubans are divided between believing their elders and supporting the revolution, and wanting to see changes in the way things are done. They would like to have the right to disagree with the government and express themselves through alternative political parties. Most want a more open economy; very few want to return to pre-revolution society.

INTERNET LINKS

Note: the official Cuban government website, **www.cubagob.cu** is available only in Spanish; likewise the site of the Communist Party of Cuba, **www.pcc.cu**.

www.cia.gov/library/publications/the-world-factbook/geos/cu.html
The CIA World Factbook page on the Cuban government includes basic facts.

www.cubaminrex.cu/en
The official website of the Ministry of Foreign Affairs is available in English.

index.rsf.org/#!/index-details/CUB
Reporters Without Borders evaluates press freedom in Cuba.

ECONOMY

A sugarcane field in Rene Fraga, Cuba

4

CUBA HAS A CENTRALLY PLANNED, or command, economy. That means all or most industry is owned by the government, which sets prices and wages. The government determines the production and distribution of goods and services. However, Cuba has been unable to provide completely for itself, and has had to rely on subsidies from other nations. Prior to 1991, Cuba's main benefactor was the Soviet Union. The collapse of the Soviet economy that year not only broke up the Soviet Union but also ushered in a difficult new era for Cuba.

Before the revolution, Cuba was a major sugar producer and tourist destination. It was economically quite dependent on the United States, which imported most of Cuba's sugar products. Visitors, primarily from the United States, came to the island for its casinos and nightlife. Most of the lucrative businesses were foreign-owned, including sugar estates and refineries. Many Cubans worked for low wages, suffered poor health, and received little, if any, education.

After the revolution, public education, health care, and mandated minimum wages vastly improved the lot of poor Cubans. The government

expropriated foreign business holdings, including US-owned sugar estates and casinos. The United States imposed a trade embargo on Cuba in the hope of crippling the new government. The Soviet Union filled the void and offered Soviet petroleum for Cuban sugar, which prompted Cuba to grow even more sugarcane.

THE US ECONOMIC EMBARGO

Cuban coins

The United States first imposed trade restrictions on Cuba in 1960, a year after Castro took power. By 1963 these were extended to include a full embargo on trade and the prohibition of all US dollar transactions with Cuba.

About thirty years later, new restrictions were proposed. The Cuban Democracy Act of 1992, sponsored by Congressman Robert Torricelli, tightened economic sanctions against Cuba in an attempt to weaken Castro and hasten his downfall. Following that came the 1996 Helms-Burton Act, which extended the trade ban to all foreign companies doing business in the United States.

The embargo was relaxed slightly in 2000, allowing US food companies to sell to Cuba. In a very unpopular move in 2004, President George W. Bush capped remittances of money to Cuba from Cubans living in the United States. Observers claim that these were efforts to bankrupt Cuba of precious foreign currency reserves. The United States maintained it would only relax restrictions when Cuba releases its political prisoners and when there are free presidential elections in the country. However, the international community largely stopped observing the embargo, leaving the United States isolated in this regard. Tourists from Canada and the European Union flock to Cuba, and their companies and governments invest, buy, and sell there.

In 2014, the United Nations General Assembly demanded an end to the embargo for the twenty-third consecutive year. US actions run counter to international opinion as expressed by the United Nations and such trade bodies as the World Trade Organization (WTO), but so far there have been no binding decisions to force the United States to back down. The saddest consequence of the embargo has been that ordinary Cubans often lack basic goods, such as medicine and food. The accumulated economic damages of the blockade are estimated at $1.1 trillion.

EL TIEMPO ESPECIAL (THE SPECIAL PERIOD)

Following the Soviet collapse in 1991, Cuba faced a sudden shortage of food, petroleum, and equipment. The threat of starvation and an increase in poverty were very real. Cuba entered *el Tiempo Especial* (ayl tee-AYM-poh ay-spay-see-al), or the Special Period, a sort of economic martial law introduced by Castro. Strict rationing was implemented to ensure that what goods were available were fairly distributed. A number of reforms were initiated to reduce the degree of dependency on imported goods.

Cuba also changed its food production in a way that attracted much attention for its success and novel techniques. Faced with a sudden loss of the chemicals and machinery supplied by the Soviet Union, Cuba worked hard to grow its own food without using much pesticides, fertilizer, or machinery. Large tracts of land, most of which were previously used to grow sugarcane and tobacco for export to the Soviet Union, were parcelled out and used to grow other crops that met Cubans' food needs.

In 1993, new legislation allowed citizens to hold and spend US dollars in a bid to save the economy after the Soviet collapse. This encouraged the currency, tourism, and remittance businesses. By the late 1990s money remitted to Cuba from abroad became the backbone of Cuba's income. The legislation was repealed after ten years in an effort to reduce Cuba's dependence on US dollars.

On the international scene Cuba sought investment from abroad and changed its laws to allow foreigners to once again own Cuban land or businesses. The main investors in joint ventures are from Spain, Canada, and Italy. Cuba's other trade partners include the Netherlands, France, Mexico,

Venezuela, China, and Russia. These joint ventures have revitalized industry, created jobs, and pumped much-needed foreign currency into the battered Cuban economy. Most of the investments have been directed at the expanding tourism market, which is the largest foreign exchange earner in Cuba. There are also other innovative partnerships, which include a joint venture to turn Cuba's natural gas byproducts into electricity and a partnership with a European company to market Cuban tobacco.

THE VENEZUELA CONNECTION

Today, Cuba still finds itself in an economically weak position, dependent—or interdependent—on other nations, notably Venezuela. Under President Hugo Chavez (in office 1999—2013), Venezuela formed a close alliance with Cuba. Venezuela gave Cuba $18 billion in loans, investments, and grants. In addition, it sold oil to Cuba at greatly discounted prices. In 2005, that amounted to some ninety thousand barrels of crude oil a day.

In exchange, Cuba sent about thirty thousand to fifty thousand technical workers to Venezuela—including physicians and other health care professionals, sports coaches, and teachers. The Cubans worked primarily in Venezuela's poverty-stricken regions. Cuba also worked to train Venezuelan doctors. Under the program *Convenio de Atención a Pacientes* (Convention Patient Care), implemented in 2000, Venezuela sent patients for medical treatment in Cuba, with the Venezuelan government paying travel costs and Cuba providing all other expenses. In 2005, for example, some fifty thousand Venezuelans went to Cuba for free eye treatment.

AGRICULTURE

Cuba is fortunate because it is the largest country in the Caribbean and most of its land is low, flat, and fertile. As the primary resource of this comparatively small country, land ownership is vital to economic well-being. After the revolution, the government expropriated foreign-owned estates and set upper limits on how much land a single owner could control. It also

distributed land to former agricultural laborers so that they received rights to land they had farmed for generations.

At a roadside market, farmers can sell their extra produce.

SUGAR Cuba was once the world's leading exporter of sugar. Sugarcane was grown on large estates retained by the government, which was about 75 percent of all agricultural land. As part of the agricultural reform in 1993, these estates were broken into smaller units and leased permanently and for free to cooperative work groups. These cooperative farms, or Basic Units of Cooperative Production, are required to produce quotas of essential crops. Once those quotas are fulfilled, they can grow any crops they like and sell them. The cooperatives get to keep the profits from these sales. Sugar is still king, but other crops are grown in larger quantities now.

In a move to diversify the nation's agricultural base, in 2002, the government reduced the acreage devoted to sugarcane by 60 percent. In its place, much of the acreages was given over to vegetable farms and cattle ranches.

RICE, CORN, POTATOES, AND CASSAVA These are leading crops in Cuba, and are grown mostly in the western part of the island. Rice, in particular, is a staple in the Cuban diet, where the national dish is rice and

SUGAR IS NOT ALWAYS SWEET

Sugar production has long functioned as the backbone of Cuba's economy, and until 1991 the export of sugar to the Soviet Union and Eastern Europe accounted for over 75 percent of the island's revenue from trade. Cuba's imports were worth $8 billion because of the favorable price the Soviet bloc was prepared to pay. Today Cuba can only sell its sugar at world market prices, and the result has been a forced reduction of imports.

Since the days of Spanish rule the Cuban economy has been locked into the sugarcane industry. For a long time the industry's high level of profitability was linked to the easy availability of cheap hired labor. After the departure of the Spanish, Cuban farmers became independent owners of sugar farms. Too soon, however, US corporations moved in. When the price of sugar reached an all-time low in the early 1920s, large US companies were able to take over near-bankrupt farms, smaller corporations, and sugar mills. By 1930 nearly three-quarters of Cuba's sugar industry was owned by US corporations, and the plantation worker found that the European colonial master had been swapped for one nearer home.

A man squeezes juice from sugarcane.

Another problem that continues to bedevil the Cuban sugar industry—whether under Spanish, US, or Cuban control—is the unpredictability of drought. A lack of expected rain can seriously damage the value of the eventual sugar harvest. Fluctuations in world prices for sugar, combined with the adverse effects of a drought, have led planners to actively seek a more diversified economic base.

beans. However, Cuba cannot grow enough of its own rice and must import a great deal of it. Cassava is a starchy, tuberous root grown throughout the Caribbean and a major source of carbohydrates for people living in tropical regions. It is an extremely drought-resistant food source.

TOBACCO Tobacco is an important crop for Cuba. It's grown to make cigarettes for local consumption and high-quality cigars for export. In fact, Cuba is world famous for its cigars. Under the US embargo, they are banned in the United States, and are therefore all the more prestigious to American cigar aficionados.

FRUIT Cuba is the world's third-largest producer of grapefruit, but most of the island's citrus harvest is oranges. Plantains and bananas are also grown, as are mangos, papayas, pineapples, avocados, guavas, and coconuts.

OTHER INDUSTRIES

The largest industries are pharmaceuticals, petroleum, and cement. Sugar milling is the chief form of food processing, allowing for the production

A tobacco farmer collects tobacco leaves.

One of the brightest lights in the Cuban economic future is tourism. Before 1959, it was Cuba's second-biggest source of revenue. The island was infamous for its casinos and dubious nightlife, and was a convenient vacation spot for wealthy North Americans. After the revolution, all tourist hotels and casinos were closed, and the US government forbid its citizens to visit the island. The tourism industry did not recover until the mid-1970s when Canadians, Latin Americans, and Europeans—especially from Spain—were attracted to the beautiful island that was far less expensive than most of its Caribbean neighbors. Since the late 1980s, increasing the number of visitors has become a national priority.

Until 1997, contact between tourists and regular Cubans was forbidden. The Cuban tourist industry operated in complete isolation from normal Cuban society. However, the government backed down somewhat in the face of global complaints. In 2008, President Raúl Castro ended the policy of restricting certain hotels and services to tourists only.

Cuba is being marketed as an ecologically friendly island with plenty of natural attractions. Its white sand beaches, rolling mountains, historic architecture, and lively culture have strong tourist appeal. Many natural areas have been preserved in Cuba, and with the incentive of tourist revenue, the country is committed to protecting them in the future.

Cuba's tourist capital is the beach resort town of Varadero, but there are also many other destinations competing for the nearly 3 million visitors that arrive each year. The growth of the tourism industry has been phenomenal. Normalizing political relations with the United States, should that occur, will have a tremendous impact on Cuba's tourism sector, and the opportunities for Cuba's economic growth in general will expand greatly.

not only of raw sugar but also such byproducts as brandy, rum, and molasses. Approximately 17 percent of the labor force is employed in the industrial sector.

FISHING Being an island nation, Cuba has an important fishing industry. Since 1959 Cuba has expanded its fishing industry with subsidies from the Soviet Union. The industry was heavily affected by the Soviet Union's collapse but has since picked up momentum. The Cuban government has taken steps at the national, regional, and local levels to make fisheries more sustainable. It also supports state-of-the-art aquaculture facilities. Meanwhile, Cuban fishing fleets operate from Greenland to Argentina. Major exports include lobsters, shrimp, and fish.

MINERALS Like other Caribbean islands, Cuba is not particularly mineral-rich, but it has more than 10 percent of the world's known nickel reserves. Nickel is the second-largest export item after sugar. Copper, chromium, and cobalt are also mined, as well as lesser quantities of salt, lead, zinc, gold, silver, and petroleum.

INTERNET LINKS

www.globalsecurity.org/military/world/cuba/economy.htm
This is a good overview of Cuba's economic situation.

www.npr.org/sections/thesalt/2014/12/18/371478629/what-the-change-in-u-s-cuba-relations-might-mean-for-food
This article focuses on Cuba's food needs.

www.nytimes.com/2014/12/15/opinion/cubas-economy-at-a-crossroads.html?_r=0
The *New York Times* editorial "Cuba's Economy at a Crossroads" suggests ways that the United States could help Cuba.

ENVIRONMENT

The Cuban Tody is one of many colorful species on the island. It is found nowhere else in the world.

5

A S THE END OF THE US EMBARGO becomes a possibility, many people are focusing on the benefits such a move would have for Cuba. For the island's environment, however, it could be a mixed blessing. In some ways, Cuba's isolation over the last half century has helped its natural areas remain healthier than other similar places in the Caribbean. Opening Cuba to a great increase in tourism would be certain to change things.

Cuba had suffered through a long period of poor environmental awareness that resulted in a damaged environment. However, Cuban government initiatives begun in the 1990s have deepened the Cuban commitment to a healthy and sustainable environment.

DEPLETION OF NATURAL RESOURCES

When Christopher Columbus landed in 1492, about 95 percent of the island was forested. By 1900, the forest area had declined to 50 percent, and by 1959 it dipped to 13 percent. The government then implemented reforestation projects to counter this decline, and in 2010 about 26 percent of Cuba was forested.

Under Spanish and British colonization, massive clearing of land was undertaken to make way for sugar cultivation. Sugar continued to

Cuba has exceptional biodiversity—it is the most naturally diverse of all the Caribbean islands. Many of its thousands of plant and animal species are endemic, meaning they are found nowhere else.

be central to the Cuban economy during US rule, Batista's regime, and the post-revolution government. This long period of monoculture resulted in massive deforestation.

With help from the Soviet Union, Cuba built one of the most modern sugar industries in the Caribbean. Sugarcane fields were scientifically managed using fertilizers, pesticides, and herbicides, and as much of the work as possible was done using machinery. Unfortunately, these chemicals, along with the discharge from sugar refineries, contaminated waterways in Cuba. The deforested land was eroded by wind and rain that washed the soil into rivers and the sea, contributing to water pollution. Hurricanes caused more erosion and increased the salt content of the soil, therefore reducing its fertility. Cuba's many marine treasures were damaged by overfishing.

Coastal cities had little in the way of pollution control for vehicle exhaust fumes and poor solid sewage disposal management. Industrial cities, such as Havana, were highly polluted.

ENVIRONMENTAL AWAKENING

In a speech at the 1992 Earth Summit in Rio de Janeiro, Castro proposed that since the Cold War had ended, the resources that developed countries had used to accumulate arms would be better spent on fighting ecological destruction. Environmental laws and projects in Cuba increased, and Cubans became more aware of conservation issues as a result of government policies and political circumstances.

After the collapse of the Soviet Union, Cuba faced a shortage of petroleum and its byproducts, fertilizers, and pesticides. Farmers were forced to adopt organic methods, such as using animal dung and plant waste as fertilizers. Instead of chemical pesticides, farmers used integrated pest management strategies that included intercropping (growing two or more species together), crop rotation (growing different crops in succession), and relying on natural insecticides (birds, predatory insects, and plant extracts).

To address the acute shortage of food during the Special Period, as much space as possible was fully utilized for agricultural production. Even residents in cities, such as Havana and Cienfuegos, took up gardening because they were required to produce their own fruit and vegetables. They, too, were legally required to use organic methods to protect people and the environment from chemical toxins.

Machines that ran on gasoline could no longer be used, so people everywhere adopted greener alternatives. Oxen were put back in the fields, donkeys took over the highways, and bicycles filled urban streets. To meet the need for soil and fertilizer, Cuban engineers began to work on projects to recycle sewage from cities. In short, Cuba became a large-scale experiment in green living.

Many farmers have reverted to older but greener technology, like this man in Viñales, Cuba, who is plowing a field with two oxen.

Cuba has since come through the worst of the crisis due to increased tourism, agricultural diversification and innovation, and a variety of trade deals with countries that do not observe the US embargo. Official policy continues to promote green living because it saves the country from having to import fuel and expensive chemical products. Cubans also realize that part of the attraction for the millions of visitors to the island is its natural beauty, lower levels of pollution, and pristine natural areas.

RICH BIODIVERSITY

In addition to government backing at the highest level, Cuba benefits from a host of scientists, biologists, and other trained professionals who are able to address the environmental issues in the country.

Cuba is also naturally blessed with a rich species biodiversity. The country was once a land bridge between the continents of North America and South America, so the number of animal and plant species is high. Island ecosystems in the region are unique in ways biologists are still trying to understand.

Cuba has set aside 263 protected natural areas, which range from highland forests to coastal mangroves and inland swamps. There are six important wetlands and a number of World Heritage Sites, so designated for their natural significance.

THE IVORY-BILLED WOODPECKER: DEAD OR ALIVE?

The ivory-billed woodpecker was once common in Cuba. Today, however, it is probably extinct, due to the destruction of its habitat. Like its related species in the southeastern United States, the elusive bird has not been seen in years. In fact, the last sighting in Cuba was in 1987. The last confirmed sighting in the United States was in 1951.

The ivory-billed is a big bird—one of the largest woodpeckers in the world, at roughly 20 inches (51 cm) in length and 30 inches (76 cm) in wingspan. It is black, red, and white and has a distinctive ivory-colored beak. This species was once found throughout old growth swamps in Cuba, but since it requires large tracts of mature forest, it did not fare well in the face of logging and clearing of its habitat. When the bird was sighted in Cuba in 1987, it was already thought to be extinct, so bird-watchers are hopeful that it has survived, and they regularly mount expeditions into the swamps in the hopes of seeing one. The sighting prompted the Cuban government to protect the forest where it was seen, and this area later grew into the 300-square-mile (777 sq km) Alexander von Humboldt National Park in eastern Cuba.

Although the ivory-billed woodpecker has not been sighted for several decades, the park is the bird's best chance for survival on the planet as it contains untouched ecosystems and forests. Here, pine forests grow to the edge of coastal mangroves, and a full 30 percent of Cuba's native plant species thrive.

Nevertheless, the Cuban ivory-bill is presumed to have become extinct around 1990. In 2010, researchers from Cornell University in New York announced they were ending years of searching for the bird in Florida and other southeastern areas. They concluded that even if the bird still exists somewhere, there is no longer any hope of saving it.

UNDERSEAS

Being an island nation, Cuba has a large marine environment to care for as well. Cuba has one of the healthiest and most extensive coral reefs in the Caribbean. Coral reefs are often considered an indicator of ocean health. Cuba's long isolation from mass tourism and its limited agricultural practices have largely protected the reefs from the widespread disease and death occurring close by in places like the Florida Keys, Jamaica, and Mexico.

A colorful coral garden off the coast of Cuba is alive with starfish and tropical fish.

Off the southeast coast of Cuba lies a marine protected area (MPA) called *Jardines de la Reina* ("Gardens of the Queen"). Scuba divers and scientists come from all over the world to view the pristine reef ecosystem and the vast array of fish and other sea animals. Between 10 and 15 percent of Cuba's waters are already designated MPAs. The Cuban National Center for Protected Areas hopes to increase that number to 25 percent.

INTERNET LINKS

www.edf.org/oceans/cuba-crossroads
The Environmental Defense Fund site looks at Cuba's ocean environment.

www.npr.org/templates/story/story.php?storyId=121177851
This NPR story "Scientists Work to Protect Cuba's Unspoiled Reefs" is available in audio or transcript.

www.pbs.org/wnet/nature/cuba-the-accidental-eden-video-full-episode
The PBS program *Nature* presents full episodes online of its series *Cuba: The Accidental Eden*.

CUBANS

Smiling Cuban children pose together on a quiet street in Havana.

6

CUBA IS A MULTI-ETHNIC NATION in which people of all races and ethnicities have equal rights and opportunities—at least officially. Underlying their ethnic differences are similarities that help characterize the Cubans as a people. They have a reputation for being friendly and sociable. They have a strong sense of national and patriotic pride in the achievements of the last half-century, as they have overcome the odds to survive as an independent country.

ETHNIC MIX

As more and more people of different and mixed races create families, the labels used to delineate one group from another are becoming hazier. Perhaps that is why the demographics statistics for Cuba are quite different depending on the source.

The official 2012 Cuban census reported that 64.1 percent of Cubans were white, 26.6 percent were *mestizo* (mixed), and 9.3 percent were black. Other sources say more than half of the population consists of people of mixed race. In general, the Cuban population is categorized

A genetic study in 2014 found the average overall genetic ancestry in Cuba to be 72 percent European, 20 percent African, and 8 percent Native American. Different regions of Cuba presented somewhat different genetic profiles, but all followed the same pattern. Of course, this information represents an average across the whole population and does not apply to individuals. Each person has his or her own genetic profile.

as white, black, mulatto—a mix of black and white; and mestizo—a mix of white and indigenous people.

Cubans of European, mostly Spanish, descent are classified as Creole. Black Cubans are descended directly from slaves brought from West Africa in the nineteenth century. Many have come to Cuba by way of Haiti. Indigenous people are descendents of the native people of the Americas. Chinese are a very small minority. They were brought to Cuba in the nineteenth century when the African slave trade was coming to an end. More recent immigrants to Cuba are political refugees from Latin America. Castro has always championed socialist revolutions in South America and offered a home to dissidents who have had to flee their own countries.

A woman in Old Havana looks festive in a traditional Cuban dress.

After the overthrow of socialist president Salvador Allende of Chile in 1973, for example, many Chileans fled to Cuba.

RACIAL PREJUDICE

An important tenet of Cuba's identity as a socialist state is that everyone has equal rights and opportunities. In most areas of life, egalitarian principles are working successfully. Racist attitudes do, however, still influence some aspects of Cuban life, and black Cubans are not always treated in the same way as Cubans of European descent. Skin color, rather than genetics, determine a person's identity.

Cuba's 2002 census, which asked Cubans whether they were white, black or mestizo/mulato, showed 11 percent of the island's 11.2 million people described themselves as black. The real figure is more like 62 percent, according to the Institute for Cuban and Cuban-American Studies at the University of Miami.

The higher ranks of many occupations are more likely to be filled by people of European or mixed European descent. This tendency is apparent in the tourist industry, where white Cubans are more likely to be employed as receptionists, tour guides, and waiters. Black Cubans are much more likely to be employed as hotel housekeeping staff or laundry operators. Discrimination also seems to operate in various government departments.

Young black Cubans are the most disaffected group of citizens. They suffer the same material deprivations as everyone else, but they often claim to be harassed by the authorities because of their color. The police are accused of being biased when it comes to dealing with young blacks suspected of being involved in criminal activity. Nevertheless, black Cubans are hesitant to raise the issue of race. Carlos Moore, a Cuban-born expert on race issues now living in Brazil, says a civil rights movement in Cuba would not be possible. The topic is not allowed in public discourse, he says, and black people raising the issue would be jailed.

Racist attitudes that do persist in Cuba are a legacy of the past. Before 1959 racism was an accepted fact that pervaded all areas of Cuban life. Blacks occupied lower paying jobs, and racial segregation existed in social life. It was not uncommon for mulatto parents to prevent their children from marrying black people in the hope that this would improve their social and economic opportunities.

CUBANS ABROAD

Before 1959, when grinding poverty was a way of life for many Cubans, the United States beckoned as a paradise. Most Cubans who could afford the expense and obtain legal entry left for Miami. When the Batista dictatorship collapsed in 1959, the people who fled the island were affluent Cubans who realized their privileged lifestyle would not be tolerated by the new socialist regime. The majority of this exodus of about 200,000 people went to the United States. Florida was the most popular destination, and here they formed the basis for a community of Cuban exiles. Other Cubans settled in Mexico and various South American countries.

In 1965, Castro allowed disenchanted Cubans not of military age to leave. Over the next eight years another 300,000 Cubans left for the United States. Very few Cubans left their country after that. In 1980, however, some 125,000 Cubans were ferried from Mariel in Pinar del Río to Miami in what became known as the Mariel boatlift. US president Jimmy Carter welcomed them as

Brothers to the Rescue is an organization of volunteer pilots, mostly Cuban-Americans, who fly regularly over the Straits of Florida in search of Cuban refugees. The refugees are accepted as political asylum seekers and put in touch with friends or relatives in the United States.

CUBAN AMERICANS: THE FLORIDA CONNECTION

There are Cuban communities in New York, Chicago, and Los Angeles, but Miami has the largest population of Cuban-Americans. Their numbers are increasing as more refugees make the 90-mile (144.8 km) journey from Cuba. The US Department of Homeland Security reports that more than 500,000 Cuban immigrants have entered the United States since 1990. In 2013, there were more than 2 million Cuban-Americans in the United States, up from 1.2 million in 2000.

Many of the refugees who fled during the post-revolution exodus after 1959 settled down in Little Havana, a section of Miami. Most had been property owners, business owners, and professionals back home. For decades, many of those Cubans held out the hope that they would return home once Fidel Castro had been deposed. For years, they presented a strong, united, anti-Castro political bloc in the United States. They wanted the US government to finance an invasion so that they could reclaim the property that had been confiscated by the regime in 1959. US politicians, looking for their votes, took note.

However, despite US political and economic pressures, Castro remained in power until he was an old man. Meanwhile, the Cuban-Americans had children who had never been to Cuba. And they, in turn, had children who began to identify more as

A typical Cuban restaurant is located on SW 8th Street in Miami, a focal point of the city's Cuban community.

Americans than Cubans. Over time, with each new generation, the dream of returning to Cuba faded.

Today, the younger generation tends to support a more normal, open relationship with Cuba—something the older generations opposed.

political refugees. Some of the refugees later returned to Cuba.

Since the early 1990s the number of those escaping from Cuba in small boats and rafts across the Straits of Florida has increased steadily. Many think the United States has given Cubans special treatment because they are seeking asylum from a political regime viewed as repressive. By contrast, refugees from other Latin American or Caribbean countries are categorized as fleeing deplorable conditions in impoverished economies. Many critics have decried this policy as unfair.

NATURAL FLAIR

Traditional Cuban dress is colorful and flamboyant. There is no national costume, but whenever Cubans dress up they do so with an innate sense of style and exuberance. The subtropical climate encourages the wearing of light cotton clothes. An open-necked shirt, often worn over cotton slacks, is the typical male dress. Women tend to wear form-fitting and colorful clothes.

A musician wears a typical Cuban outfit while playing traditional music in Havana.

INTERNET LINKS

www.ibtimes.com/why-cubans-are-still-risking-their-lives-flimsy-rafts-leave-island-1909877
This article from the *International Business Times* is a good look at Cuban attitudes about life in Cuba.

www.migrationpolicy.org/article/cuban-immigrants-united-states
Migration Policy Institute offers an in-depth look at Cuban immigrants.

www.pewresearch.org/fact-tank/2014/12/23/as-cuban-american-demographics-change-so-do-views-of-cuba
The Pew Research Center examines changing attitudes among Cuban Americans.

LIFESTYLE

An old Cuban man sports a straw hat and a cigar on a street in Trinidad.

7

CUBANS HAVE BEEN THROUGH hard times. Nevertheless, they manage to live decent lives and enjoy good times as well. The country's ideology stresses duty and communal effort, but the ordinary Cuban has a healthy disrespect for too much authority. The role of the state is central to many areas of life, but the value of individuality continually asserts itself. Enjoying oneself is still a national hobby. Lifestyles have had to adapt to harsh economic conditions, but adjustments are often made with imagination, good humor, and a senseof optimism.

The infant mortality rate in Cuba, 4.2 per thousand births, is lower than that in the United States (6.17 per thousand), and is among the lowest in the world.

PUBLIC AND PRIVATE

Cuba has a mixed economy with a combination of private enterprise and state-controlled businesses. State enterprises run in tandem with the private sector, which makes up for deficiencies in what the state can produce or import. While the state system still runs on rationing and centralized distribution of goods, the private system is based on

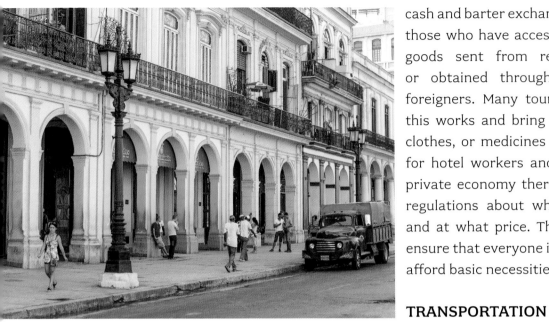

People walk past colorful buildings in Havana, making for a typical street scene.

cash and barter exchanges. This favors those who have access to money and goods sent from relatives abroad or obtained through contact with foreigners. Many tourists know how this works and bring extra toiletries, clothes, or medicines to leave as tips for hotel workers and guides. In the private economy there are still many regulations about what can be sold and at what price. These regulations ensure that everyone in Cuba is able to afford basic necessities.

TRANSPORTATION The severe shortages of gasoline in the early 1990s are now over but with the high price of oil worldwide, Cubans still restrict their use of cars. In the countryside, donkeys and horses are a common sight, and in the cities, people ride bicycles and walk when they can.

CUBAN HOMES

One positive side to Cuba's central development planning is that there are no homeless people in the country. All housing projects are initiated by the state, but tenants are able to purchase their homes through installment payments. Many Cubans become owners of their homes that way. Owners of larger houses are allowed to rent out sections as apartments. Hardly anyone lives alone in Cuba, so houses and apartments are nearly always built as family homes.

The Spanish style is clearly visible in cities such as Havana and Trinidad, where many nineteenth-century buildings are still standing. Residents in some of the older, Spanish-style buildings are forbidden from making changes to the original structures. Preserving a building's architectural integrity is not, however, the main reason for withholding improvements. Many older

MICROBRIGADES

Before 1959 poverty and deprivation were widespread in Cuba. Housing was inadequate and overcrowded, especially in cities. In the post-revolution years, an increase in the birth rate focused attention on the need for drastic improvements in the provision of housing. Cuba responded by forming microbrigades.

Microbrigades are small groups of workers who take time off from their usual occupations to assist with building programs. The workers are a mixture of professional and manual workers of both sexes. The general plan is that a section of the workforce, from a factory or government department, is mobilized to construct five-story blocks of apartments under the supervision of building professionals, while the remaining workforce maintains production levels.

In urban areas microbrigades are most likely to be engaged in public housing programs, though the focus has now shifted to tourist development and other projects. In the countryside the building brigades are involved in building new schools or homes for the elderly.

The use of these building brigades serves political and practical purposes. Cuba is intent on constructing the kind of society where all the citizens see it as their duty to contribute to the public good.

houses in the cities are crumbling and suffering from a lack of amenities, but there is not enough money to finance the repairs.

The style of old colonial buildings finds an echo in the traditional style of many rural homes. Balconies and patios are a common feature of houses in both Spain and the Caribbean. The architecture is a natural response to a hospitable climate that encourages people to think of their home as extending beyond the four walls of the house itself. People like to relax at home; sitting on a patio with friends or neighbors comes naturally to Cubans.

THE STATUS OF WOMEN

The Cuban constitution guarantees women "the same opportunities and possibilities as men in order to achieve woman's full participation in the development of the country." The nation consistently ranks high in international surveys on women's rights. The World Economic Forum's 2012 Global Gender Gap Report ranked Cuba nineteenth among 135 countries in a survey that measured the health, literacy, economic status, and political participation of women. For comparison, the United States came in at number twenty-three.

Women make up about 38.1 percent of Cuba's total workforce. It helps that the state provides childcare facilities. Places of employment usually have day nurseries, allowing infants to be looked after during working hours. Especially in the fields of law, academia, and medicine, women have attained the kind of professional success that is more commonly associated with men in most other countries. Nevertheless, Cuban women earn on average less than half what men make, mostly because men have access to higher-paying jobs. Less than 40 percent of working-age women are employed.

Management positions and government appointments are predominantly held by men. Some women employees feel that they stand lower chances of being promoted because they are undervalued by their employers. Yet others feel burdened by domestic duties and do not have the time to upgrade themselves by attending training. In general, however, women in Cuba suffer much less discrimination than women in other countries in the region.

MARRIAGE

Older Cubans remember the days when girls of marriageable age went out only when chaperoned by an older brother or relative. Courting began in the local park where girls would walk around in pairs, with arms linked around each other's waists. The boys would stroll around some distance away. Courtship was highly formal, subject to parental approval, and expected to culminate in a marriage ceremony at the local church.

During the first ten years after the revolution, the number of marriages doubled, while the rate of divorce increased eightfold. These dramatic increases reflected the radical changes affecting women and men. Improvements in economic conditions, such as the lowering of rents, increased people's purchasing power and encouraged the planning of families. The traditional role of women as homemakers was challenged as more and more women entered the workforce and benefited from equal educational opportunities. The role of religion declined, and the government established "Palaces of Marriages" across the country where secular marriage ceremonies were conducted.

Divorce laws were liberalized, and the process of obtaining a divorce became readily available to all social classes. Divorce is easy and continues to be fairly common. Cuba has one of the highest divorce rates in the world, and the highest in Latin America. Among the reasons cited for the prevalence of divorce in Cuba are poverty, increased economic responsibility for women as they join the workforce, and having to live with other family members in the same house. Cohabitation is a common occurrence. Birth control is widely practiced and abortions are relatively easy to obtain.

A young couple poses for wedding pictures in a park in Trinidad, Cuba.

EDUCATION FOR ALL

Education is one of the bedrocks of the Cuban revolution and continues to be a priority, whatever the cost. From nursery school to university, school is free for all Cubans. School transportation, textbooks, equipment, and school meals are all provided free by the state. The state maintains a student-to-teacher ratio of 12 to 1, which is half the average of other Latin American countries. As of 2010, Cuban secondary schools were striving towards a goal of only fifteen pupils per class.

Cubans must attend school between the ages of six and fifteen. The first level is primary school, which lasts six years. Then they move on to basic secondary, which lasts three years. After that they have a number of choices: quit school, continue with technical or professional training, or prepare

Legally, Cuba is committed to sexual equality. Socially, however, there is still a strong macho element in the national culture. In the machismo ethic, the female role is primarily domestic and submissive to male authority. The male role is to exercise authority and display macho aggression in both private and professional life. In other words, while men are encouraged to exhibit machismo, women are expected to conform to opposite values of virtue and demureness. Machismo is equated with masculinity itself.

The regulation that says it is a man's duty to share household chores is part of a process designed to eliminate machismo. An article of the Family Code, entitled "Rights and Duties Between Husband and Wife," is recited by the person officiating at the marriage ceremony. In addition, children are educated in a highly political way that includes an emphasis on sexual equality. Traditional attitudes die hard, however, and many Cuban males would be upset to think that

whistling or hissing at a female was anything more than a charming compliment. People joke that adultery is a national sport—for men only.

The problem is more than an annoyance, however. Because the machismo attitude reduces a woman's worth, it can be used to justify violence and crimes against women. Laws alone cannot solve the problem, and even then, sometimes the law will look the other way at so-called "family concerns." For Cubans, the debate about machismo is gaining momentum as more people question traditional gender roles.

for university. The technical or professional students can qualify after three years as skilled workers or mid-level technicians. Finishing this level qualifies them to enter technical colleges if they wish to improve their training. Students who choose to prepare for university enter a pre-university school, where they study for three years. Cuba has forty-seven universities and enrollment is about 112,000. All universities are public, of the same status, and administered by the government. Universities offer bachelor's, master's, and doctorate degrees.

A classroom of Cuban elementary school children are dressed in uniforms in 2014 in Havana.

Teachers must complete a five-year training course in either primary or secondary education. University professors must be experts in their fields, but they also receive teacher training and attend upgrading courses throughout their careers. This makes the quality of Cuban education, at all levels, one of the best in the hemisphere.

Illiteracy has been virtually eliminated. Over a million adults were taught to read and write in a literacy campaign that began three years after the revolution. Adult education remains an important part of the national system of education. There are branches of the main universities in all the provinces, and many areas have schools of music, art, and ballet. These facts represent one of the country's greatest achievements, and Cubans feel justly proud of their educational resources.

HEALTH CARE

While the Castro regimes' economic achievements have been unsatisfactory, and their record on human rights is deplorable, there are two sectors in which they shine—education and health care. All Cubans are entitled to free comprehensive health care as part of the mandate of the revolution. Cuba's quality of health care is ranked among the best in the world and is unsurpassed in Latin America. Medical training is a popular course of study,

In 2004, Cuba passed a law forbidding private citizens to access the Internet. It was illegal to buy a computer without government approval, and approval was rarely granted to ordinary Cubans. In addition, the cost of connection was high and there was limited bandwidth. On top of that, the government censors maintained a tight grip on access to Internet content. Cuba has been listed as an "Internet Enemy" by the group Reporters Without Borders since the list was created in 2006.

As a result, Cuba remains one of the least connected countries in the world, in terms of Internet connection. In 2012, only about 10 to 25 percent of the Cuban population had access to the Internet. This doesn't necessarily mean those users had access to the World Wide Web. Two parallel networks coexist on the island: the international network and a closely monitored Cuban intranet. The intranet consists only of an encyclopedia, e-mail addresses ending in ".cu" used by universities and government officials, and a few government news websites such as Granma. Many users could not access the www.

In 2015, in response to President Barack Obama's overtures toward normalizing relations with Cuba, things began to change. The Cuban government announced it would expand Internet access and lower the cost. The state-run telecommunications company, Etecsa, opened thirty-five Wi-Fi hot spots around the island, mainly in parks and boulevards of cities. The cost was set at $2 per hour, half the price of a connection in an Internet café, but still out of reach for most Cubans.

How much the Cuban government lifts censorship remains to be seen. However, officials seem ready to acknowledge that restricted Internet access is hurting the country's economy. Executives from both Google and Twitter quickly approached the Cuban government about offering their services there.

and the education system has produced an abundance of physicians, both generalists and specialists.

Fidel Castro was twice awarded the Health for All medal from the World Health Organization (WHO) and was the first head of state to receive one. He received the first medal in 1988 for achieving health standards in Cuba that WHO had set as goals for developing countries by the year 2000. Cuba met these targets in 1983, seventeen years ahead of schedule. In 1998, Castro earned the second medal for having more Cuban doctors serving abroad than the WHO itself had and for reducing infant mortality considerably.

Cuba is often the first country to respond to a medical crisis in the world, sending doctors, nurses, mobile hospitals, and vaccines whenever it can. Due to the US embargo on trade in medicines to Cuba, the country established its own biomedical research industry in the mid-1980s. This industry produced the first meningitis-B vaccine. Today it exports a low-cost hepatitis-B vaccine to more than thirty countries and is developing anti-cancer therapies. With even tighter restrictions on imported medications today, Cuba has turned to expanding its knowledge and use of natural remedies.

A scientist works at the Center for Genetic Engineering and Biotechnology in Havana in 2013. The center is a leader of Cuba's biotechnology sector for oncologic, autoimmune, infectious disease, and cardiovascular projects.

INTERNET LINKS

academicexchange.wordpress.com/2015/01/08/15-facts-on-cuba-and-its-education-system
This site offers an informative list of facts about education in Cuba.

en.rsf.org/internet-enemie-cuba,39756.html
This is the Reporters Without Borders page regarding Cuba and the Internet.

www.huffingtonpost.com/salim-lamrani/cubas-health-care-system-_b_5649968.html
This article says Cuba's health care system is a model for the world.

RELIGION

Thousands of Roman Catholics in Cuba mark the end of Holy Week with religious processions, now fully sanctioned by the government.

ROMAN CATHOLICISM IS CUBA'S largest religion, but the numbers of believers are hard to pin down. Although the Catholic Church estimates between 60 and 70 percent of Cubans are Catholic, only 5 percent or less attend Mass regularly. Compounding that, much of Cuban Catholicism today is modified by Santería, a syncretic Caribbean religion. Santería blends elements of Catholicism and West African beliefs in a way that makes it difficult to pry the two apart for statistical purposes. In any event, most Cubans are not particularly religious.

"I read all the speeches of the pope, his commentaries, and if the pope continues this way, I will go back to praying and go back to the church, and I'm not joking." —President Raúl Castro, May 2015, after meeting with Pope Francis at the Vatican

CATHOLIC CHURCH AND STATE

Article 8 of the Cuban constitution proclaims that "the State recognizes, respects, and guarantees religious freedom." The Cuban government does not, however, do anything to encourage the influence of the Catholic Church in Cuban life. Under the Spanish, the Church was part of the colonial establishment and consequently lost favor with many people. After the Spanish, but long before the revolution, there was

growing disenchantment among Cubans about the way the Church failed to champion the needs of the poor who made up the majority of the population. Some priests did, however, speak out against the injustices under the Batista regime. In fact, a Catholic priest served as a chaplain with the revolutionaries in the Sierra Maestra. Catholics and priests also served as members in Castro's revolution.

People pray during Mass on Easter morning, April 5, 2015. The Methodist Church of Marianao in Havana had fewer than 400 members in the late 1990s, and has more than 3,200 today.

As the country became more socialist, the Catholic Church became more hostile. In 1960, the rule of Castro was formally denounced in a pastoral letter that was read out at all services. Castro responded by declaring, "Whoever betrays a revolution such as ours betrays Christ and would be capable of crucifying him again."

In the 1960s, the power of the Church was regulated by the new government. The number of priests was reduced by 70 percent, and church schools were replaced by ones that excluded any religious education.

Many of the churches do not conduct religious services and function mainly as places of architectural interest. For a long time it was considered incompatible for a Cuban to hold allegiance to the Church and to the revolutionary State.

In the 1990s, the government relaxed its attitude toward the Church, perhaps because the Church has unbent a little from its anti-government position. The 1992 amendment to the constitution included a ban on religious discrimination and allowed practicing Catholics to become members of the Communist Party. Since the collapse of the Soviet Union observers have noticed an increased interest in all forms of religion by Cubans. This may be related to the harsh economic climate.

Fidel Castro was baptized and raised a Catholic but never practiced the religion as an adult. In 1962, Pope John XXIII excommunicated Castro because of his oppression of the Church in Cuba. After that, Castro was not merely a nonpracticing Catholic, he was not a Catholic at all—which suited him just fine.

After the revolution, Cuba was officially an atheist nation. Though the government did not officially ban religious practice, it did actively discourage it. In the 1990s, the years following the collapse of the Soviet Union, Castro relaxed restrictions on religion and shifted the country status from officially atheist to officially secular. By then, only about 2 percent of Cubans attended weekly church services.

In 1998, Pope John Paul II visited Cuba at Castro's invitation. While he was there, the pope severely criticized the US embargo. Not long after the pope's visit, Castro restored Christmas as a national holiday. During his time in Cuba, John Paul II blessed a stone that was to stand at the entrance to the first new seminary to be built since the Cuban revolution. The seminary opened in 2010, five years after John Paul's death.

In 2012, Pope Benedict XVI made a three-day visit to the island and met with President Raúl Castro and former President Fidel Castro (below). The pope celebrated Mass in Santiago's Revolution Square before about two hundred thousand people.

In September 2015, Pope Francis was scheduled to visit Cuba. The pope played an important role in brokering the 2014 Cuba–US deal to restore diplomatic relations. In May 2015, Raúl Castro met Francis in the Vatican to thank him. Castro was so impressed by the pope that he quipped he might return to the faith he was born into.

AFRO-CUBAN RELIGIONS

The thousands of slaves transported to Cuba by the Spanish brought their religions with them. The Catholic Church was tolerant toward these non-Christian beliefs, partly because the African religions were receptive to some aspects of Catholicism, and a synthesis of sorts took place.

Pedro Agustin Morell de Santa Cruz, a bishop of Cuba between 1753 and 1768, witnessed a rebellion of slaves and saw good reason for tolerating some aspects of African theology. If some tolerance was shown, he thought, there would be less resentment by the slaves and in time their beliefs would wither away. Under Morell, the Christian celebration of Epiphany (January 6) became a festival for slaves where they were allowed to elect symbolic chiefs and perform religious dances.

It is possible that church authorities were misled as to the extent and depth of this synthesis. Catholicism never took deep root among Cubans, while the African religions flourished and spread to non-black Cubans. Today forms of Afro-Cuban religions are commonly practiced by Cubans of all ethnic origins. There are no official figures, but as many as half to three-quarters of all Cubans subscribe to Afro-Cuban beliefs.

When white Cubans began to attend ceremonies in large numbers a catchphrase developed to explain their presence: *"Yo no creo pero lo repito"* (yoh noy KRAY-oh PAYR-roh loh ray-PEE-toh), or "I do not believe but I repeat the ritual."

SANTERÍA

Roman Catholicism is being increasingly challenged by Santería, an African religious cult that includes aspects of Catholicism, notably saint worship. The literal meaning of *Santería* is "the way of the saints," and the religion is traced back to the Yoruban region of Nigeria in West Africa, the original home of the first slaves destined for Cuba. Over the centuries Santería has mixed its Yoruban spirit worship and magic practices with those from other parts of Africa, especially the Cameroons, and Cuba's neighbor Haiti. The most potent mix, however, has been with Spanish Catholicism.

The rituals of Santería are very secretive and open only to initiates. Its primary liturgical language is Lukumí, a late 1800s dialect of the Yoruban language interspersed with elements of Cuban Spanish. Santería worships hundreds of gods and goddesses, but about a dozen have emerged as more important to contemporary Cubans. The primary ritual associated with Santería is a dance accompanied by drum music. Dance allows the participants to imitate and role-play events from traditional stories about the lives and deeds of the gods. Different types of drums have special qualities, often magical ones, and are associated with certain gods.

The traditional place of worship is the *cabildo* (ka-BEEL-doh), a cross between a church and a drinking club. While some aspects of Santería's devotional practices are remarkably Christian in character, others are recognizably African. It is not uncommon for mass hysteria to develop at large gatherings, and devotees, convinced of being possessed, may dress in the clothes associated with their god.

Voodoo puppets play a role in Santería.

ORISHA The gods and goddesses of Santería are called *orisha* (hor-ISH-ah). They are also known as saints. This is a result of the synthesis that occurred when the African beliefs absorbed some aspects of Catholic theology and practice. Christ became Olofi and the Virgin Mary is associated with Yemaya, goddess of the sea and mother of the orisha and the world. Acts of homage are made by slaughtering animals. Important deities are closely identified with certain colors. Ochun, or Oshun, is a beautiful goddess whose color is yellow. She is known for her sexual conquests and yet manages to merge

A Cuban man, a follower of the Palo religion, draws a magical symbol on the floor of the temple in Santiago de Cuba.

with Caridad, the Christian patron saint of charity, who is also renowned for her virginity, and who is also Cuba's patron saint.

People choose a particular orisha to worship and display their allegiance by wearing beads of the orisha's color around the neck or wrist. Like the Christian saints, each orisha has its own special date that functions as an anniversary. The anniversary calls for acts of adoration, and a devout believer keeps a shrine at home and decorates it colorfully on that day. Small symbolic offerings of food are laid at the foot of the shrine, candles are lit, and prayers are said.

Two other African religions practiced in Cuba are Palo Monte and Abakua. Palo Monte, also known as the Mayombe cult, originates from the Bantu people of what is now Angola. Adherents of this secretive religion are referred to as *paleros* (pa-LAYR-rohs) or *congos* (KOHN-gos) and undergo an initiation ceremony. In common with contemporary beliefs of Bantu people in Africa, there is a strong reliance on the power of black magic, and this characterizes many of the rites.

A religion open to males only is Abakua. It originates from Nigeria and Benin in Africa, although at the present time the majority of its adherents in Cuba are white Cubans. Some observers play down the spiritual aspects of the religion, claiming that self-interest rather than theology binds the members together. It has been compared to the Mafia in terms of its influence and methods. An obligatory part of the initiation ceremony once involved the new member killing the first person he met. Presumably, that is no longer the case.

There are no established places of worship for these religions, and while they are tolerated by the government, they do not receive any official support. Abakua, especially, is viewed with some suspicion as a potentially subversive group.

A "Nianigo," a member of the Abakua brotherhood, dances with the head of a chicken in his mouth during a ceremony. It is the conclusion of a two-day initiation rite for new members in the town of Cardenas in the Matanzas province of Cuba.

INTERNET LINKS

santeriachurch.org
The Santería Church of the Orishas site is maintained by a California denomination, and offers good explanations in English.

www.cubaabsolutely.com/AboutCuba/articles_religion.php?id=Santeria-The-African-roots-of-Cuba
On the Cuba Absolutely website, this and other religion articles are very interesting and informative, with many photos.

www.washingtonpost.com/blogs/worldviews/wp/2015/04/10/cubans-love-the-pope-and-the-catholic-church-but-theyre-just-not-that-into-religion
This *Washington Post* article is about the results of a poll on religious practice in Cuba.

LANGUAGE

A signpost shows directions to famous landmarks in Havana.

9

THE MOST OBVIOUS LEGACY of Cuba's colonial past is the Spanish language. First came the conquistadors, missionaries, and sailors; then the merchants and farmers. All spoke Spanish and permanently imposed their language on the island. A similar process occurred on other Caribbean islands and in most of Latin America.

The March 2, 2015, issue of *Granma*, the Cuban daily newspaper

A young tourist couple takes in the sights of Old Havana on the Plaza de la Catedral.

Today Spanish is spoken by all Cubans and is also the language of government and commerce. English, Cuba's second language, is taught in all the schools and required for entrance to university. Russian used to be taught in schools, but it was never very popular. Many Cubans learned Russian when they traveled to the Soviet Union to be trained as scientists and engineers.

The growing importance attached to tourism has increased the use and appeal of English among many Cubans. In this sense a cycle has been completed, for before the revolution, English was widely spoken for the same reason. Older Cubans who had been involved in the lucrative US tourist trade are finding that their second language is once more in demand.

SPANISH PRONUNCIATION

Pronouncing words in Spanish is easy because basically all the letters are pronounced, subject to some clear rules. The letter *h* is never pronounced, so the capital of Cuba is pronounced ah-BAN-ah. The letter *j* is pronounced as an

People play the chess on central square in Santiago de Cuba.

aspirated (meaning, pronounced breathily) *h*, so the popular male name José is pronounced hoh-SAY.

The same rule applies to the letter *g* when it is followed by an *e* or *i*. For example, the word *gigante* ("giant") is pronounced hee-GAN-tay. When speaking Spanish there is little difference between the letter *v* and the letter *b*, so the word *vino* ("wine") is pronounced BEE-noh.

CORRECT STRESS Knowing where to place the stress in a word is governed by a systematic rule. Words ending in a vowel or *n* or *s*—the majority of words in Spanish—always receive a stress on the next-to-last syllable. For instance, the word for president, *presidente*, is pronounced pray-see-DAYN-tay. All words that end in any consonant except *n* or *s* always receive the stress on the last syllable. If a word breaks this rule and is to be stressed on any other syllable, the change is signified by an accent over the vowel to be stressed. Guantánamo, for example, is pronounced gwan-TAN-a-moh, while *Guantanamero* (a citizen of Guantánamo) is pronounced gwan-ta-na-MAYR-roh.

One mark above a letter that affects pronunciation is the tilde. This is a small wave above the *n* that appears in words like *España* ("Spain") and *mañana* ("tomorrow"). It changes the sound of the letter *n* to *ny* so that the word for tomorrow is pronounced man-YA-na.

CUBAN SPANISH

The first Spaniards to settle in Cuba came from the southern part of Spain known as Andalusia. Although centuries have passed since they first arrived, they have left a deep influence on the way Cubans speak Spanish. A chief characteristic of Cuban Spanish is the relaxation of consonants, especially at the end of words, and the running together of words. While this is a general characteristic of Spanish in Latin America, it is particularly noticeable in Cuba. Visitors who speak European Spanish often find the pronunciation in Cuba more difficult to adjust to than in other Spanish-speaking countries in Latin America and the Caribbean.

In European Spanish the letters *ce, ci,* and *z* have a soft *th* sound. A word like *cerveza*, meaning "beer," is pronounced thayr-VAY-tha as if the

English	Cuban-Spanish	Pronunciation
Hello	*Hola*	oh-la
Goodbye	*Adios*	ad-ee-OHS, final *s* very slightly pronounced
Pleased to meet you	*mucho gusto*	MOO-choh GOO-stoh
I am hungry	*tengo hambre*	TAYN-goh AM-bray
I don't speak Spanish	*no hablo español*	noh AB-loh ay-span-YOHL
United States	*Estados Unidos*	ay-STAD-ohs oo-NEE-dohs, final *s* of both words, very slightly pronounced

speaker has a slight lisp. Cubans tend to drop the *th* sound altogether and replace it with an *s* sound, sayr-VAY-sa.

A characteristic of Cuban Spanish is the tendency to drop the pronunciation of the *s* at the end of words. This is becoming increasingly common throughout Latin America. Linguists predict that it is only a matter of time before the final *s* sound is eliminated altogether. It is natural to wonder, then, how the plural is distinguished from the singular. In the case of a word like *la mamá* ("mother"), usually the context makes it clear whether one mother or a group of mothers (*las mamás*) is being referred to. Both words are pronounced ma-MA.

An old classic taxi passes a revolution sign on a street in Havana in 2013.

FORMS OF ADDRESS

In Spain the terms *señor* (sayn-YOR) and *señora* (sayn-YOR-a) are the common forms of address corresponding to Mr. and Mrs. These terms are used in Cuba but are regarded as rather formal. People generally prefer to use the term *compañero* (kohm-pan-YAYR-roh) or *compañera* (kohm-pan-YAYR-ra), both of which mean "comrade."

Cuban surnames consist of two words, but it is only the first surname that is usually used. For example, the name of the country's president is Raúl Castro Ruz, but to Cubans and the rest of the world, he is referred to as just Raúl Castro. The unused part of the surname, Ruz, is his mother's second name.

When women marry, their third name, that is, the second part of their surname, is replaced by de followed by the husband's second name. If Miss María Suárez Prieto married Mr. Pedro Raul Maurell, for instance, she would become Señora (Mrs.) María Suárez de Raul. As the third name is reserved for strictly formal occasions, by both men and women, it is usually not obvious from a woman's name whether she is married. The surname of Señora María Suárez Raul's children would be Raul Suárez.

Cuba is a highly politicized country, and this is reflected in the use of banners, posters, and slogans to communicate political ideas. Poster art is highly developed in Cuba, usually accompanied by words but equally capable of communicating successfully through visuals alone.

During the 1960s, particularly, the use of posters to communicate with citizens was an aspect of daily life. The images were mounted in special poster stands and periodically changed, in the way that advertising posters are changed in the United States and other countries. Posters that were regarded as particularly successful in communicating ideas about political and social issues were reproduced in books and presented on billboards. Giant billboards erected before 1959 to carry advertising campaigns now bear provocative images about international solidarity.

When Cuba faced the threat of imminent invasion by US-backed counter-revolutionaries in the 1960s, the political motto Patria o Muerte *(PA-tree-a oh moo-AYR-tay)—"Country or Death"—was frequently used to instill a sense of patriotism and solidarity. The threat of invasion has since diminished, but the economic crisis has caused the motto to evolve into* Socialismo o Muerte—*"Socialism or Death."*

The most iconic poster that Cuba has produced is that of revolutionary rebel Che Guevara. Posters of Guevara are found everywhere in Cuba, and his images have been reproduced on various items, such as key chains, matchboxes, and coins.

Street names also bear testimony to political attitudes. In the first year of Castro's rule, many changes were made to the names of main streets that dated from the colonial influence of Spain and the United States. This tradition has continued. In 1973, for instance, Avienda Carlos III—named after a Spanish king—became Avienda Salvador Allende to commemorate the socialist president of Chile, who was deposed shortly after his election.

BODY LANGUAGE

Using body language as a form of expression is an integral part of the Cuban communicative process. It is often used in an almost intuitive manner. For example, when a Cuban wants to refer to Fidel Castro the gesture of rubbing an imaginary beard will sometimes be used instead of his name or title. No ridicule or contempt is implied by such a gesture.

The natural use of body language is also apparent in Cubans' frequent handshaking. In many Western countries the handshake is often a formal gesture of politeness, but Cubans will use it as a measure of their intimacy with the other person. If the relationship is a close one the handshake will often be correspondingly elaborate. Friends of both sexes also greet each other with a kiss on both cheeks.

Cuban women greet each other in the customary way.

INTERNET LINKS

www.cubaabsolutely.com/AboutCuba/article_customsL.php?id=Lost-in-Translation
Cuba Absolutely offers this article about a non-Cuban trying to learn the cultural fine points of Cuban language.

www.donquijote.org/culture/cuba/languages/cuban-spanish
This is another quick look at Cuban Spanish.

www.veintemundos.com/en/spanish/cuba
This site offers a quick overview of language in Cuba.

ARTS

A Cuban musician looks sharp as he plays the trumpet.

10

THE RICH AND CREATIVE SIDE OF Cuban culture is most apparent in the arts. Cuban music is a popular form of art for non-Spanish speakers, and together with dance, it expresses an essential aspect of Cuban identity. The visual arts are equally compelling.

A young percussionist plays Cuban drums in an evening concert.

Cuba's most beloved song and unofficial anthem is "Guantanamera." There are several versions, but the "official" lyrics are based on poetry by the national hero José Martí. During the time of the Cuban missile crisis, US folksinger Pete Seeger reworked the traditional version to emphasize peace and recorded it on his 1963 album, *We Shall Overcome*.

CUBAN MUSIC

A festive occasion in Cuba not accompanied by music would be unimaginable. Listening and dancing to music comes naturally, for Cubans possess a rich musical tradition. Cuban singers and bands have a strong following in Latin America, and many of Cuba's top musicians regularly tour foreign countries. Professional musicians are employed by the State, and highly talented individuals receive the highest salaries.

The unique sound of Cuban music harks back to the music's origins in the Yoruban and Congolese cultures of West Africa, the original home of many Cuban ancestors. It accounts for the distinctive use of percussion instruments and for the strong link between music and dance and the practices and beliefs of Santería.

Cuban bands usually have at least one guitar player. The Spanish introduced the guitar, and with the instrument came the dramatic, vigorous Spanish flamenco sounds. Spanish influence also accounts for ballad singing.

THE MUSIC OF SON (SOHN) CUBANO, the indigenous dance music of Cuba, is one of the most influential and widespread forms of Latin American music. It goes back at least two centuries to its home in eastern Cuba. The soul of son music is African, but the Hispanic musical tradition has contributed to its evolution. The three distinguishing characteristics of son music are the rhythm tapped out on two heavy wooden sticks called claves, the solo vocal element requiring improvisation by the singer, and a repeated chorus toward the middle or end of the musical piece.

Cuban musicians Roberto Hernandez "Roberton," (right), and Juan Formell (left) of Los Van Van perform at Karl Marx Theater on December 9, 2009 in Havana. Bassist Formell, the band's leader, died in 2014.

A wide range of musical instruments is used in son, including the organ, accordion, flute, violin, trombone, and even the synthesizer. One of the lesser-known instruments used is the *tres* (TRAYS), a small three-string guitar. The tres produces a delicate, metallic timbre, one of the most recognizable sounds of son.

Son-changüi (SOHN-chan-GWEE) was one of the earliest forms of son music that originally combined the tres, bongo, and maracas. Through the twentieth century, other instruments, such as the trombone, were added to it. Elio Reve was a son-changüi musician who, in the late 1960s, was inspired to combine his music with *son-charanga* (SOHN cha-RANG-a) forms and instruments. Son-charanga is an early twentieth-century form of son that adopted European influences and such instruments as the violin, woodwinds, and flute. Son-charanga combines a strong African- and Spanish-influenced rhythm with flute, violin, and piano improvisations. Elio Reve joined forces with Juan Formell in 1969 to form Los Van Van and create a new sound called *songo* (sohn-goh). Songo combines trombones, violins, and Cuban percussion with American funk, rock, and jazz sounds to create a vibrant sound.

BUENA VISTA SOCIAL CLUB became internationally famous with the recording of the album *The Buena Vista Social Club*, produced by Ry Cooder, in 1997. This album revived interest in traditional Cuban music among younger Cubans as well as worldwide. It features some of Cuba's best son singers and musicians, such as Compay Segundo, Eliades Ochoa, Ibrahim Ferrer, and pianist Rubén González. The release of this album was such an international hit that a documentary movie was made of it in 1999. The film, also called *Buena Vista Social Club*, was produced by German director Wim Wenders and nominated for an Academy Award for Best Documentary Feature. Some of the band members were quite old by the time the acclaim brought them back into the limelight, and several passed away shortly afterward—Segundo at age ninety-five, González at eighty-four, and Ferrer at seventy-eight. The group's signature piece, which is on the album, is "Chan Chan," written by Compay Segundo in 1987.

ALL THAT CUBAN JAZZ   Cuban rhythms have influenced jazz since its birth, and from the 1930s the effect was especially decisive. The Dizzy Gillespie Orchestra's popularity was enhanced by the incorporation of Cuban sounds in 1946. A few years later, Stan Kenton, a prominent jazz musician, hired drummers from an Afro-Cuban band to make a hit record, *The Peanut Vendor*. After World War II, New York and Cuban jazz deeply influenced each other. Today, Cuban jazz takes many forms that depend on the major rhythm adopted. Famous names include Chucho Valdés, his group Irakere, and acclaimed pianist Gonzalo Rubalcava.

HIP-HOP AND REGGAETON   Hip-hop is very popular. It first found its way into Cuba in the 1990s by way of US radio transmissions. At first the Cuban government was not very happy with the form, which features a great deal of political and social commentary. However, Cuban hip-hop

SALSA

Salsa music is derived from son and was brought by self-exiled Cubans to the United States, where it is currently enjoying a revival. It is far less pure than son, having absorbed extraneous rhythms such as soul and rock, and salsa fans are not conscious of its Cuban origin. Cubans discuss music in terms of how sabroso *(sa-BROH-soh), or tasty, it is. This may explain the word* salsa *("sauce"). The characteristic sound is a combination of fast piano pieces and multiple percussion instruments. If the band is a big one, guitars, horn, and double bass are added. The result is a small orchestra resembling the big bands that dominated the 1950s cabaret scene in Havana. Those who first exported salsa include members of such orchestras.*

and rap have evolved as distinctive from the US style, and the government appears to have accepted it. Some notable groups are Orishas, Cubanito 2002, and Explosión Suprema. The popular rap duo Los Aldeanos, on the other hand, has incurred official displeasure with some "anti-socialist" lyrics. Though the group has a huge fan base in Cuba, most venues refuse to book it.

Reggaeton is another matter. A popular mix of hip-hop, reggae, and Latin beats, it is a blatant and aggressive style that is often criticized as vulgar and obscene. In 2012, Cuban officials banned the style in public spaces, because they said it demeans women as "grotesque sexual objects."

DANCE

Dance is as integral to Cuban culture as music is, and dancing the night away often literally describes what happens when Cubans are out to enjoy themselves. As with music, the origins of Cuban dance lie in both Africa

In the 1960s, The Beatles were banned from Cuban radio. Today, Havana's Parque Menocal has been renamed Parque John Lennon (John Lennon Park) and features a sculpture of the former Beatles member, created by Cuban artist José Villa Soberón.

and Spain. In Catholic-run colonies, drum music and dancing by slaves were not regarded as morally unhealthy or politically dangerous as was sometimes true in the Protestant areas of the southern United States. Consequently, the intricate rhythms accompanying religious rituals were better preserved.

The link between music, dance, and religion is especially preserved in rumba, a form of music that originated among the communities of poor blacks in Havana around the turn of the century. It has been called the purest form of African music to have survived in Cuba.

Traditional rumba music takes different forms. The *yambú* (yam-BOO) is a relatively slow dance performed by two dancers. The *columbia* (koh-loom-BEE-a) is usually a men's dance and sometimes involves the use of machetes and knives. It is faster and more exciting than yambú and originates from the Matanzas region. The country's most famous rumba group is known as Los Muñequitos de Matanzas.

Other forms of popular dancing in Cuba can be traced back to Spain and France. The traditional French country dance known as *contradanza* (kohn-tra-DAN-sa) was introduced from Haiti. A slower Cuban version, equally classical and formal, is called *danzón* (dan-SOHN) and is related to the cha-cha. Dance forms like the cha-cha, conga, mambo, and tango are performed with artistic verve in Cuba.

Alicia Alonso performs in New York City in 1975.

BALLET Ballet is also highly regarded in Cuba. The National Ballet Company ranks as one of the world's most talented dance companies and once had close links with the Bolshoi and Kirov ballet companies of Russia. The most prominent ballet personality in Central America is Alicia Alonso (b. 1921), a Cuban. She studied in Cuba and New York, where she made her professional debut. She was financially unsuccessful in running her own ballet company in Havana in the 1940s and left once again to work in New York. After the 1959 revolution, she returned to Cuba and directed the National Ballet Company, which was given government subsidies.

Two other important dance companies in Cuba are Camagüey Ballet and Cuban National Dance.

PAINTING

One of Cuba's most famous artists is Wilfredo Lam, who was part of the post-World War II surrealist movement. One of his works, *La Jungle*, is in the Museum of Modern Art in New York. In paintings, he set out, in his own words, "to paint the drama of my country, but by thoroughly expressing the Negro spirit, the beauty of the plastic art of the blacks."

Lam died in 1982, but a contemporary artist, Manuel Mendive (b. 1944), is consciously building on a similar Afro-Cuban aesthetic. He incorporates African saints into his rich, colorful works. His surrealistic, jewel-toned work, *Se Alimena Mi Espiritu* ("My Soul is Nourished") (2007), for example, portrays Oshun, the orisha of the river, love, and prosperity. Mendive is said to be the most important Cuban artist living today.

Raúl Martínez is the painter who introduced pop art into Cuba. In *The Island*, painted in 1970, he presents a group portrait of anonymous Cuban citizens alongside such prominent individuals as Castro, Che Guevara, and the North Vietnamese leader Ho Chi Minh. Its political message is that all

Untitled (1970) by Wilfredo Lam reflects the influence of the Spanish artist Pablo Picasso, who was a friend and teacher of Lam's.

Cuban writer and diplomat Alejo Carpentier poses in 1979 in Paris.

Cuban people are equally important, and no one person should have a special heroic status. Martínez also paints posters, and one of his most famous calls for the end of machismo.

LITERATURE

Several generations of Cubans grew up studying European and American literature but were not exposed to their native literary traditions. Cuban literature existed, but not many educated Cubans appreciated it.

After 1959, when the revolutionary government took over, Cubans were encouraged to read books with themes of revolution or equality. Students of Cuban literature are encouraged to read Cirilo Villaverde's *Cecilia Valdés*, a novel about an ill-fated romance between a mulatto woman and a Spanish-Cuban aristocrat.

Contemporary writers, like all other artists in Cuba, work independently but are salaried by the state. A number of literary competitions are held annually, and winning writers are guaranteed the publication of their book. A highly literate population in a remarkably politicized country provides a very sophisticated readership. It also promotes a healthy literary climate that nurtures new writers and sustains established ones.

Important writers include the novelist Alejo Carpentier (1906–1980) and the poet José Lezama Lima (1910–1976). The novels of Carpentier, a former journalist and diplomat, belong to an era of political ferment and have wide international appeal. They include *Kingdom of the World*, *Explosion in a Cathedral*, and *Reasons of State*. Lima's poetry is more concerned with a search for the roots of Cuban identity. His most important work, *Paradiso*, has been translated into English.

Political thrillers are very popular with Cubans. In 1974, when two writers wrote the mystery thriller *The Fourth Circle*, the first print-run of eighty thousand copies sold out within one month. One of the writers, Luis Rogelio Nogueras, later wrote a novel, *If I Die Tomorrow*, which had a plot involving a Cuban secret service agent infiltrating a group of anti-Castro terrorists.

POETRY

Poetry's wide appeal is shown by the regular publication of poems in newspapers and magazines. The nationalist hero of the nineteenth century, José Martí, is also a revered poet. Children are first introduced to his romantic lyric poems in school. A respect for poetry is an accomplishment that most Cubans maintain throughout adult life.

> *With the poor of the earth*
> *I am happy with my lot:*
> *The mountain stream*
> *Pleases me more than the sea.*
> *—José Martí, "The Temple of the Mountain"*

Nicolás Guillén, a mulatto born in 1902, was one of the Caribbean's best-known poets. He was Cuba's poet laureate until his death in 1989. Other poets, such as Nancy Morejón, have achieved recognition. Morejón combines romantic themes with revolutionary commitment and echoes the work of José Martí.

FILMS

One of the major artistic developments since 1959 has been the successful creation of a thriving film culture. The government set up the Cuban Institute of Film Art and Industry, which was largely responsible for starting this development.

In the 1960s and 1970s, full-length movies often had considerable artistic merit, as well as being free of ideological control by the government. Several Cuban films have received acclaim at international festivals, including *Memories of Underdevelopment* by Tomás Gutiérez Alea and *Lucia* by Humberto Solás, both of which were produced in 1968.

Strawberry and Chocolate, by Alea and Juan Carlos Tabio, won the Special Jury Prize at the 1994 Berlin International Film Festival. Juan Carlos Cremata's *Nothing* received recognition at the 2003 Miami International Film Festival when it received the jury's Grand Award.

An art installation by Kcho, a well-known Cuban artist is on exhibit in May 2015 at the Havana Biennale.

More recently, notable Cuban films that won international acclaim and awards include *Habanastation* (2011) by Ian Padrón; *El Ojo del Canario* [The Eye of the Canary] (2010), by Fernando Pérez, which is based on the childhood and adolescence of José Martí; and *Fuera De Liga* [Out Of The League] (2008), a baseball documentary by Ian Padrón.

ART FESTIVALS

Every other December, Havana dances to the sounds of the International Jazz Festival. Aficionados of jazz from all over the world descend on the city and join over a thousand Cuban fans for a festival of listening, dancing, and drinking rum. Jazz festivals are held all over the world, but the annual event in Havana inspires particular respect among devotees of this type of music.

Non-jazz music festivals are held annually at the tourist resort town of Varadero on the north coast. These include the Varadero International Music Festival and Electroacoustic Music Festival.

The Habana Bienal (Havana Biennial) is an important international arts festival that features exhibitions of paintings, other art forms, and conferences, and is an expression of Cuba's commitment and support to Third World cultural development. Latin American artists provide two-thirds of the total work shown.

Cuba also sponsors the annual International Festival of the New Latin American Cinema. It is a prestigious event that brings together filmmakers and critics from all over the world. People come not only to view new films but also to attend conferences and critical debates on film theory and practice. Hollywood figures occasionally attend, and past guests have included Francis Ford Coppola. The festival usually opens in the grand, old-style Hotel Nacional in Havana.

Equally prestigious, but in the field of ballet, is the annual Havana International Ballet Festival. It was started in 1960 and continues to attract major ballet companies from all around the world.

INTERNET LINKS

www.boogalu.com/features/history-cuban-music
Boogalu Productions offers a good overview of the history of Cuban music.

www.buenavistasocialclub.com
This site tells the story of Buena Vista Social Club, with photos, to the track of "Chan Chan" in the background.

www.cuba-culture.com/cuban-dance
Cuba-culture has a quick guide to Cuban dance styles.

www.visitcuba.com/2012/01/30-of-the-best-contemporary-cuban-movies-2006-2011
Visit Cuba lists "30 of the Best Contemporary Cuban Movies (2006—2011)" with descriptions.

Two men play a board game in Trinidad, Cuba.

I N A SOCIALIST SOCIETY, ACCORDING TO Marxist theory, leisure time is to be used in a constructive, educational manner to create "the new man"—the communist citizen. To that end, Cuban authorities encourage workers to spend their free time in valuable social activities. Sports, especially, are considered activities that can prove the ideology of the Cuban political system.

BASEBALL

Baseball is Cuba's most popular sport. The game was introduced to the island from the United States in the nineteenth century, although evidence suggests that indigenous tribes like the Cuban Taínos played a ball game similar to baseball. The game of batey was played by the Taínos on a stone-lined paved court.

Before 1959 the best teams in Cuba were linked to US leagues. Scouts of top US teams regularly searched Cuba for young players to sign. Many turned out to be highly talented players who later made successful careers with major league teams. A Cuban pitcher for the Cincinnati Reds, Dolf Luque, was with the team for more than a decade. He was the first Cuban-born player to play in the major leagues. Other famous Cuban players of the period leading up to the revolution include Minnie

11

The Cuban flag flies in the outfield as kids play baseball in in the Alamar suburb of Havana in May 2015.

Minoso of the Chicago White Sox and Camilo Pascual of the Washington Senators.

Despite the severing of relations with the United States, there has been no drop in Cuban enthusiasm for baseball. It remains the national sport, and every large town has a stadium that fills up for baseball games. The rules are exactly the same as those in the United States, but there are some surprising differences. No fee is charged for admission to a game and fans are likely to cheer teams with cries of "Socialismo o Muerte" ("Socialism or Death")!

Cuba's national team was always a contender for a medal at the Olympic Games. Indeed, it took home gold medals in 1992, 1996, and 2004. The team lost to the United States in 2000. (Since then, baseball has no longer been an Olympic sport.) Cuban players can also be found on professional teams in the United States, where high salaries are a definite attraction.

Weekends are the time to play with young and old. Amateur and professional players turn out to fill the many baseball parks and stadiums around the country. Every school competes in interschool leagues, and local community groups organize their own competitions.

PLAYING THE GAME

Cubans engage in many other games besides baseball. Basketball comes a close second in popularity. The seventeenth Caribbean Basketball Championships were held in Cuba for the first time in 2004. Both the Cuban men's and women's teams emerged as the winners. In 2006, 2007, and 2009, Cuba took a bronze; and in 2014, Cuba took a silver medal in that competition.

A tradition of playing chess is still upheld in Cuba. A youngster may first learn the game in junior high school, and public chess tables in parks are often used for games between senior citizens.

Rows of jai-alai cestas, the long, curved wicker scoops used by player to catch and throw the ball, sit in shelves.

Historically, soccer was not a top sport in Cuba, but in recent years, its popularity has soared. In June 2015, the New York Cosmos soccer team played against Cuba's national team in Havana. It was the first US professional team to play in Cuba since Presidents Raúl Castro and Barack Obama announced that they were re-establishing diplomatic relations.

Tennis, squash, wrestling, fencing, swimming, rowing, and volleyball are some other popular sports usually first encountered in school. Wrestling and fencing are particularly popular, and on weekends there is usually a match in a town gymnasium. Even a small town has at least one gymnasium. Often a temporary ring is set up in a town square to host a local tournament.

A three-walled court game enjoyed immensely by players and spectators alike is jai alai, which came to Cuba from the Basque region of Spain. It is a very fast game, for two or more players, that depends on quick reflexes and speed. Using a 2-foot (0.6 m) wicker basket strapped to the hand, players try to hit a small hard ball against the front wall of the court so that their opponents are unable to return it and thus lose a point.

Track and field, along with baseball and boxing, has made Cuba internationally famous. National teams regularly take first place in the Central American and Caribbean Games, and are often the favorites to win events at the Pan American Games. Cuba can also be guaranteed to return from the Olympics with a cluster of gold, silver, and bronze medals.

This tradition existed in Cuba before 1959, when it was mainly the sport of middle- and upper-class men. After the revolution, when the sport was nurtured by the state and made available to all classes, its popularity increased.

Over the years, Cuba has produced some outstanding boxers, including featherweight Kid Chocolate (Eligio Sardinias Montalbo) and welterweights Kid Gavilan (Walter Gerardo Gonzalez), Benny Paret, and Luis Rodriguez. The most successful was Teofilo Stevenson, who was three times Olympic heavyweight champion—in 1972, 1976, and 1980.

Cuban boxers are frequent medal winners at the Olympic Games. In the 2012 Summer Games in London, for example, they took home two golds and a bronze.

As in other sports in Cuba, there is no clear-cut distinction between amateur and professional players. There are no professional athletes; however, the government attaches a lot of importance to sports, both as a form of fitness and leisure as well as a source of national pride and achievement. Talented individuals are encouraged to devote themselves full-time to a particular sport. During this time they receive a salary and in many respects function as professionals.

Boxing is first introduced to young boys at school. Those who show skill and interest are usually encouraged to train by preparing for a local tournament. The country's major boxing competition is the Giraldo Cordova Cardin Tournament, and leading boxers are expected to prove themselves at this annual event.

THE ART OF RELAXING

The art of relaxing is an attractive aspect of Cuban culture that finds expression in a variety of ways. A rocking chair is a common item on the verandah or balcony of a Cuban home. People like to sit in the comfort of their homes and pass the time of day with like-minded neighbors or family acquaintances. Friendship and friendly conversation are highly regarded in life.

Even more emblematic of contentment is the picture of a relaxed individual seated in a comfortable rocking chair and smoking a Cuban cigar. The enjoyment of a fine cigar is regarded by tobacco users as deeply satisfying, and Cubans are blessed—as well as cursed, in terms of the damage to their health—by ready access to the best cigars in the world. Fidel Castro was a dedicated smoker for many years; he was invariably featured holding a huge cigar in his hand or mouth. In his own words, "after a truly heroic struggle," he managed to quit the habit, but for many Cubans leisure time without a cigar is unthinkable.

Cuban cigars, especially the better quality ones, used to be very popular in the United States but can no longer be sold there because of the embargo. In addition, tobacco smoking of all sorts has grown far less popular in the United States because of concerns about tobacco-related health issues.

A NIGHT OUT

A *casa de la trova* is a cross between a bar, a dance hall, and a small concert hall. These centers are open from around 9 p.m. to midnight. They are very popular on weekends, when they also are open during lunchtime. Most large towns and cities have a casa de la trova.

A *trova* is a classical ballad. In the past, troubadours traveled from town to town to recite their ballads to the accompaniment of music. Traditional troubadours are still to be found, but today the range of songs and music is far wider. The *nueva trova* (new-ABE-a TRO-ba) has introduced post-revolution themes into the songs, and there is a blues version of the *trova* known as *filin* (FIL-in). Distinguished

CUBAN CIGARS

The Taíno tribes smoked tobacco and passed the habit on to the Spanish settlers, who in turn introduced the idea to Europe. As smoking became increasingly popular and fashionable, the foundations for Cuba's cigar industry were laid. The reputation for excellence associated with Cuban and especially Havana cigars is unrivaled anywhere in the world. Famous personalities, such as American writer Ernest Hemingway, who lived for years in Cuba, extolled their virtues. Other famous Cuban cigar enthusiasts included American comedian Groucho Marx and British prime minister Winston Churchill.

The majority of cigars are machine-produced, but rolling a cigar by hand is still a highly regarded skill. All cigars bear a colored ring that denotes their quality. Cuban men choose a cigar because of its strength and flavor. The word oscuro *(os-KUR-o) means dark, but when applied to cigars it means black and very strong;* maduro *(mad-UR-o) means ripe, and this describes a brown-black cigar with full-bodied flavor;* colorado *(kolo-RAD-o) means red, and is a reddish-brown, aromatic cigar;* claro *(KLAR-o) means clear, and denotes a mild-flavored cigar.*

Cigar aficionados also claim that the size and shape of a Cuban cigar affect its flavor. Apart from the very popular torpedo, named after its shape, there is the corona cigar with straight sides and one end closed. The perfecto is cylindrical and tapered, with a half-pointed head.

Cigar factories have a tradition of entertaining and educating cigar makers as they work by having readers recite passages from books. Another tradition is that employees smoke freely as they work and take home a couple of cigars each day. The average life expectancy for Cuban men is about seventy-six, but it is a lot shorter for cigar makers. Cuba sets high quality standards for its cigars, and this limits the number of cigars it produces.

Cuban troubadours include Faustino Oramas and Pedro Luis Ferrer.

A lot of entertainment available to Cubans in their leisure time is free of charge. There is no admission fee to attend a sports event or enter a casa de la trova. Places that do charge admission, such as the cinema and theater, are not run as profit-making businesses. The cost of a ticket to see a movie or a play is a far smaller proportion of a person's income than it is in the United States or Europe. As a consequence, cultural establishments like theaters are patronized by a wide cross-section of the population.

Perhaps for this reason, the distinction between highbrow and popular culture does not apply in Cuba. Places of entertainment that are often associated with particular income levels in other countries are frequented by Cubans of all classes.

A performer sings at the Tropicana Cabaret in Havana.

INTERNET LINKS

www.baseballdecuba.com/?language=en
Baseball de Cuba, the website of the Cuban national baseball team, is available in English.

www.cnn.com/2012/05/23/sport/olympics-2012-cuba-boxing/index. html
CNN presents the article "The Secrets to Cuba's Boxing Success."

FESTIVALS

A Cuban man drums during a street festival in Old Havana.

12

FESTIVALS AND HOLIDAYS PLAY AN important role in Cuban life, even though most of them have been around for only about fifty years. When Fidel Castro took power, he abolished many of the public holidays and replaced them with new ones that commemorated important events in the country's history.

The most dramatic consequence of these changes was the demise of religious festivals that had once played an important role in the social life of Cubans. The desire to celebrate did not disappear but was channeled into the new holidays that marked achievements important to all Cubans. Living with economic uncertainties means people cannot spend as much money as they used to, but the spirit of enjoyment remains undiminished.

REMEMBRANCE OF THE NATIONAL REVOLUTION

Havana and Santiago de Cuba put on the most colorful celebrations for Cuba's major annual festival on July 26. Cubans pour into these cities from the countryside to join in the festivities. For weeks before, people are busy preparing fantastic costumes and making the floats that are a highlight of the parades. Across the island, groups of people based around a place of work, an organization, or a residential district strive to produce the most flamboyant and eye-catching displays. A sense of

Every year on May 1, the celebration of Labor Day, more than a million people gather at the Plaza de la Revolución in Havana, to rally at the foot of the giant statue of José Martí, the Cuban national hero.

Hundreds of Cubans wave the national flag expressing support for Fidel Castro and Raúl Castro during the annual celebration of the Cuban Revolution in 2008.

pride accompanies these efforts, and tremendous enthusiasm is generated.

Dancing is an essential part of the celebrations. While some dance troupes are professional, the majority are formed by local groups that practice and rehearse with amateur musicians. Dance and music are integral parts of Cuban culture enjoyed by young and old. Even when economic conditions are bad, Cubans come out on July 26 to sing and dance and enjoy themselves. Traditionally, an abundance of food accompanies street parties. Vendors set up stalls selling barbecued pork, a Cuban party favorite, barbecued goat, and whistles and party favors for children. Along with a plentiful supply of rum and beer, these mark the occasion as a special celebration.

CARNIVAL

The July 26 national holiday coincides with a traditional carnival that goes back a long way in Cuban history, as far back as 1493, when Christopher Columbus visited Cuba a second time, bringing sugarcane from the Canary Islands.

Cuba's most important holiday lasts from July 25 to July 27. Known as Remembrance of the National Revolution, this period celebrates an event that took place six years before the actual overthrow of Batista. On July 26, 1953, a group of about 150 revolutionaries led by Fidel Castro launched an attack on the Moncada Barracks just outside the city of Santiago de Cuba. Militarily, the attack was a dismal failure. The rebels had neither the experience nor the weapons to successfully capture the army post, and many of them were shot and killed by Batista's army. Others were captured and tortured to death. Castro escaped but was captured a week later and imprisoned. Ironically, the failed attack was to prove successful in its ultimate aim of igniting a revolutionary spirit among Cuban people. Black and red flags began to appear marked M•26•7, indicating the birth of the Movement of July 26, and the struggle against Batista was resumed with renewed determination.

July 26, along with the day before and after, is a national celebration across Cuba. Posters and flags appear long before the day, still bearing the legend M•26•7, and festival events are organized in every community. What helps to make the event so spectacular an occasion is that this part of the year had been a festive occasion long before the attack on the Moncada Barracks. Previously, it marked the time of the important sugar festival and was traditionally a time for relaxation and celebration. This was why the rebels chose July 26 for their attack; they hoped to catch the soldiers unprepared and too drunk to fight back.

Before the advent of machine harvesting, all the sugarcane had to be cut by hand using wide-bladed machetes. It was a back-breaking and exhausting occupation. Once the cane was cut, the workers could enjoy a period of rest, and because this was the time they received their wages, it was natural to celebrate.

The workers on the sugar plantations were originally all slaves from Africa, and the dances and music of Carnival can be traced back to traditional tribal festivities from West Africa. Havana and Santiago de Cuba are the most important places where these traditional celebrations are actively preserved. In Santiago de Cuba there is even a museum devoted to preserving memories and artifacts connected to the songs and dances of the July carnival. The drum is especially prominent in Carnival celebrations in Cuba.

PUBLIC HOLIDAYS

July is by no means the only time when Cubans celebrate. There are four other official holidays, all of which have a political significance. These days are marked by a mixture of public speeches and partying.

Cuban President Raúl Castro participates in a ceremony in Santiago de Cuba marking the fifty-fifth anniversary of the Cuban Revolution on January 1, 2014.

Political leaders deliver keynote speeches to vast crowds of supporters. Such speeches are usually held in large open spaces, such as the Plaza de la Revolución in Santiago de Cuba. The atmosphere at these gatherings is genuinely festive. Both before and after the speeches the crowds are entertained with songs, dance, and music.

The celebrations are extended to evening time, when parties are organized both inside and outside people's homes. There is usually a lot to eat and drink at these parties to contribute to the merry atmosphere.

Public holidays are also occasions for families to come together. January 1 is the most important day of the year in this respect. The first day of the year happens to coincide with the date of dictator Fulgencio Batista's departure from Cuba in 1959, and so it functions as an anniversary of the birth of the new regime.

Notwithstanding its political significance, New Year's Day has always been a special day in Cuba. The last day of the year, December 31, is not an official holiday, but it tends to resemble one because so many people take the day off work to prepare for parties that night.

FEBRUARY 24

Another important political anniversary is commemorated every February when large posters celebrate the anniversary of Cuba's Second War for Independence.

Plans for the February 24 rebellion were laid as early as January 5, 1892, when José Martí established the Cuban Revolutionary Party in New York, where he lived in exile. He and other exiled rebel leaders held several meetings in Jamaica and Costa Rica, and completed their plans on Christmas Day 1894. On February 24, 1895, uprisings began all over Cuba. The war lasted a few years. It cost the lives of Cuba's most colorful revolutionaries, but it achieved freedom for Cubans with the creation of the Republic of Cuba on May 20, 1902.

Soon after Fidel Castro took power in 1959, he declared the new Communist Cuba to be an atheist nation. Christmas was no longer observed as a holiday–in fact, it was banned. For most people, it became just another ordinary day. Those who did continue to celebrate Christmas did so in a quiet, muted manner.

Things changed in 1998, when Pope John Paul II visited Cuba. For the pope to make such an official visit was an extraordinary thing in itself. He convinced Castro to restore the Christmas holiday. In 2012, Pope Benedict XVI visited Cuba and succeeded in having Good Friday re-instituted as well.

Today, Christmas in Cuba is still not a major celebration—after all, the younger generations of Cubans grew up without Christmas traditions. Nevertheless, December 24 is a time for family feasts and parties. With the thaw in US–Cuba relations, however, and the lifting of travel restrictions, it's quite possible that Christmas traditions will be revived, if only to draw tourists.

In any event, December is a relatively merry time in Cuba, with jazz, conga, and rumba festivals, street parades, the annual Havana Film Festival, and New Year's Eve, which is a very popular occasion.

RELIGIOUS DAYS

Traditional religious festivals have either been completely abandoned or absorbed into days of secular celebration. January 6 used to be the celebration of the Feast of Kings, commemorating the day when the Three Kings brought gifts to baby Jesus. Parents used to buy small surprise gifts for their children and presented them on the morning of January 6. Although the day now only has special significance for the small minority of Christians in the country, the tradition of exchanging gifts has not completely died out. However, it is more common for gifts to be given and received on July 26.

Cuban pilgrims arrive at the Sanctuary of St. Lazarus in El Rincón on December 17, 2014. They dress in purple to celebrate one of the island's most important religious rites, the pilgrimage to pay homage to the saint of healing.

Before 1959 the most important religious festival was Holy Week, the week before Easter. In 1965 Holy Week was changed to Playa Giron Week and became the focus for periods of mass voluntary labor. Playa Giron is a small village very close to the site of the failed Bay of Pigs invasion, which took place over the Easter period in 1961. In 1969, the Easter period became the Playa Giron Month, part of a campaign to increase the country's production of sugar. Currently it is known as the Playa Giron *Quince* (KEEN-say), meaning Fifteen, to signify a two-week period of communal effort.

INTERNET LINKS

www.cubagrouptour.com/information/cuba/events
This tourism site offers an overview of annual festivals in Cuba.

www.usatoday.com/story/news/world/2014/12/25/cuba-havana-christmas/20897667
This is an interesting article about Christmas in Cuba.

FOOD

Sofrito—made of finely chopped peppers, onion, and garlic with oregano—adds flavor to many Cuban dishes.

13

CUBAN CUISINE IS A TASTY MIX of Taíno, Spanish, African, and Caribbean flavors and techniques. It bears a strong resemblance to the cuisines of neighboring Dominican Republic and Puerto Rico. Rice and beans, either together or separately, form the basis of many meals. The flavor foundation of *sofrito*—onion, green pepper, garlic, and oregano—is used in many dishes. Cuban cookery is mainly a peasant cuisine of simple, unfussy dishes that rely on local ingredients. Root vegetables such as yuca, managa, and boniato are common staples, along with plantains.

CUBAN TASTES

Cuban tastebuds are not as attuned to hot food as in some neighboring Latin American countries. There is a partiality for spicy tastes, but compared to nearby Mexico, the result seems mild. Nevertheless, a pork chop, for instance, would never be prepared without a mixture of different spices being fried at the same time. Beans of various sorts are

● ● ● ● ● ● ● ● ● ● ● ● ● ●
The Cuban government runs restaurants for tourists, and for the most part, their reputation for quality dining has not been the best. Beginning in 1990, however, the law has allowed small, family-owned restaurants called *paladares*. These offer home-style Cuban food and are often located in people's homes.

a regular favorite. *Congri* (KOHN-gree), or rice and beans, is made with kidney beans, but black beans and white beans are also used.

Before the food shortages made any sort of meat expensive, a favorite meat was chicken. Crocodile meat is sometimes eaten, and the taste, somewhere between that of chicken and pork, is not exotic. Turtle meat is used to prepare stews and soups. Pizza is very popular as a quick lunchtime meal.

RICE WITH EVERYTHING

The most basic Cuban food item is rice. It forms the staple of most meals and is commonly served with beans. *Moros y cristianos* (MOHR-rohs ee kree-stee-AN-ohs)—Spanish for "Moors and Christians"—is the name given for a popular dish of white rice and black beans cooked together. The dish is named Moors and Christians because the ingredients are black and white. In medieval Spain, the Moors were Arab Muslims, typically dark-skinned, and the Christians were white. Another rice dish that is as popular in modern Spain as it is in Cuba is *arroz con pollo* (a-ROHS kohn POHL-yoh), chicken with rice.

Picadillo (pee-ka-DEEL-yoh), Spanish for minced meat, uses ground beef mixed with green peppers, onions, tomatoes, and olives. Raisins are often mixed in with the rice, and sometimes a fried egg is laid over the rice.

CUBAN DRINKS

The most popular alcoholic drink at social and festive occasions is rum. The drink is distilled on the island and used to be widely available to all Cubans. Today the rum and beer produced on the island is mainly for export or tourist consumption.

The lively *cervecerías* (sayr-vay-sayr-REE-as), the equivalent of a bar or pub once found in almost every town, are now rarely open, and the production

Moros y cristianos (black beans, rice, and fried ham), is a favorite dish in Cuba, as well as in the West Indies and Central America.

Since the effects of the US embargo on trade were first felt in Cuba, the government has rationed basic goods. Ration books, called libretas *(lee-BRAY-tas), are given to each household according to the number of adults and children to be fed. The rationing system not only ensures an equitable distribution of limited goods, but also functions as a welfare program. Each month, every Cuban receives a basic basket of food for less than $2.*

In recent years, that monthly supply has been seven pounds of rice, half a bottle of cooking oil, one sandwich-sized piece of bread per day, plus small quantities of eggs, beans, chicken or fish, spaghetti, white and brown sugars, and cooking gas. Children under seven receive one liter of milk a day. People with special needs get ration booklets designed for their situation. Cubans pick up their monthly allowance of supplies at a government run food pantry called a bodega.

Prior to 2009, many non-food items were also rationed, such as detergent, cigarettes, house supplies, toys, and even rum, but these have since been removed by President Raúl Castro. In fact, Castro wants to do away with the entire system, as he sees it dragging down the Cuban economy. The country spends around $1 billion annually on rationing, subsidizing 88 percent of the cost. The

Cuban food ration book

rations are not enough to live on, however, and Cubans must supplement with groceries bought on the open market.

Will the resumption of diplomatic ties between Cuba and the United States lead to an invasion of US fast food chains on the island? Some people are worried that it will, and the influx of burger, pizza, and fried chicken joints will ruin the Cuban street scene. Others think the increase in US tourists will probably mean the demand for US-style fast food will rise, and that there's simply no way to avoid it.

Small, private cafés in Havana and some of the other cities already offer versions of these sorts of foods. Pizza is well known in Cuba; there are plenty of smaller, fast food places. Cuban pizza usually has a very doughy crust with a goopy sauce and cheese topping and is served as small individual pies on wax paper. The toppings, if there are any, are typically baked under the cheese rather than on top of it

The quality of the pies is debatable, however; it's normal for the restaurant to simply microwave a frozen pizza as the customer waits.

Until recently, all of Cuba's pizza joints were government owned, which meant the quality was mediocre. People got used to it. But the new movement toward small private restuarants called *paladares* is creating new "pizza paladares." Cuban chefs are finding information on top-quality pizza-making on the Internet, so it might not be long before Cuban pizza sheds its old, blah reputation.

of drinks for domestic consumption has been drastically curtailed. The same is true even of the *guaraperas* (gwa-ra-PAYR-ras), bars selling drinks of freshly pressed sugarcane. Ironically, the juice of the one crop that Cuba produced in abundance is no longer available to the Cuban people. There was a time when crowded places, such as train and bus stations, attracted mobile stalls dispensing sugarcane juice and a pineapple-based drink known as *piña fría* (PEEN-ya FREE-a).

Coffee is the most popular hot drink. It is drunk from tiny cups and is often sipped with ice water. Unlike regular North American coffee, it is quite thick and syrupy. Every town has its share of kiosks and stalls serving only coffee, and many customers bring their own cups to be filled, often improvised from cut-down beer cans.

The most popular tea in Cuba is the herbal variety. Many towns have shops specializing in the preparation of herbal drinks. The dark, orange pith of the tamarind pod, for instance, produces a popular beverage after it has been soaked in sugary water for three or four days. The pod of the tropical African baobab tree is also used in an herbal drink. Herbal drinks can be traced back to Africa, where their medicinal properties were the source of their popularity.

INTERNET LINKS

www.cbsnews.com/news/cuba-economic-reforms-felt-at-the-dinner-table
This story discusses how the Cuban food rationing system affects everyday life.

www.cubanfood.org
This site offers a wide range of recipes for what it calls "genuine Cuban cuisine."

www.tasteofcuba.com
This is a recipe and restaurant guide.

ROPA VIEJA (SHREDDED BEEF)

In Spanish, the name means "old clothes," because the beef is shredded until it resembles old rags. It is traditionally served with white rice.

3 lbs (1350 grams) flank steak, cut into strips (or use skirt steak or chuck steak)
4 Tbsp (60 milliliters) olive oil
5 cloves garlic, minced
1 medium onion, sliced
1 red pepper, sliced
1 Cubanelle, poblano,
   or green pepper, sliced
1 Tbsp (15 mL) cumin
1 tsp (5 mL) dried thyme
2 tsp (10 mL) oregano
1 bay leaf
6 oz tomato paste
1 cup (240 mL) white wine
1 ½ cups (350 mL) beef stock
1 cup (240 mL) can whole
   peeled tomatoes, crushed
¼ cup (60 mL) fresh cilantro,
chopped
salt and pepper to taste

Season the beef with salt and pepper. In large pot or skillet, brown it on all sides in oil. Remove from skillet. Add the onion, garlic, and peppers to pan and cook over medium heat until soft, about 4 minutes. Lower heat, add spices and tomato paste; cook about 3 minutes. Add wine; cook, scraping bottom of pot, for 1 minute. Return steak to pot with stock and tomatoes; boil. Reduce heat to medium-low; simmer, covered, until steak is very tender, 2—3 hours. Remove steak and shred. Return to pot and cook until sauce is slightly thickened, about 30 minutes. Remove bay leaf. Stir in cilantro before serving. Serve with white rice. Serves 6.

CUBAN FLAN

This caramel custard is a favorite dessert in Cuba.

½ cup (120 mL) sugar
1 tsp (5 mL) water
1 whole egg
5 egg yolks
1 (12 oz.) can evaporated milk
1 (14 oz.) can sweetened condensed milk
1 tsp (5 mL) vanilla

Preheat oven to 350 degrees Fahrenheit.

First, make the caramel. In a small nonstick saucepan, heat the sugar and water over medium heat. Shake and swirl occasionally to distribute sugar until it is dissolved and begins to brown. Do not stir. Use a pastry brush dipped in water to wash the sides of the pan free of granular sugar. When caramel is dark golden brown, immediately pour it into a glass casserole dish or a loaf pan, and swirl to coat the bottom and sides. (Watch carefully! Caramel burns quickly!)

While caramel cools, make the custard. In a separate bowl or in a blender, beat the egg and egg yolks together. Add the evaporated milk, sweetened condensed milk, and vanilla, and mix together. Pour the custard mixture into the casserole dish over the hardened caramel.

Place the dish into a water bath—place in a larger baking pan and fill the larger pan with hot water to about half-way up the sides.

Bake in a pre-heated 350-degree oven for 45 minutes. Turn off the oven and let set for another 15 minutes. Remove from the oven and the water bath and let cool.

To plate, run a knife around the outside edge of the flan. Place a plate large enough and deep enough to catch the liquid caramel and invert. Chill the flan for at least an hour before serving.

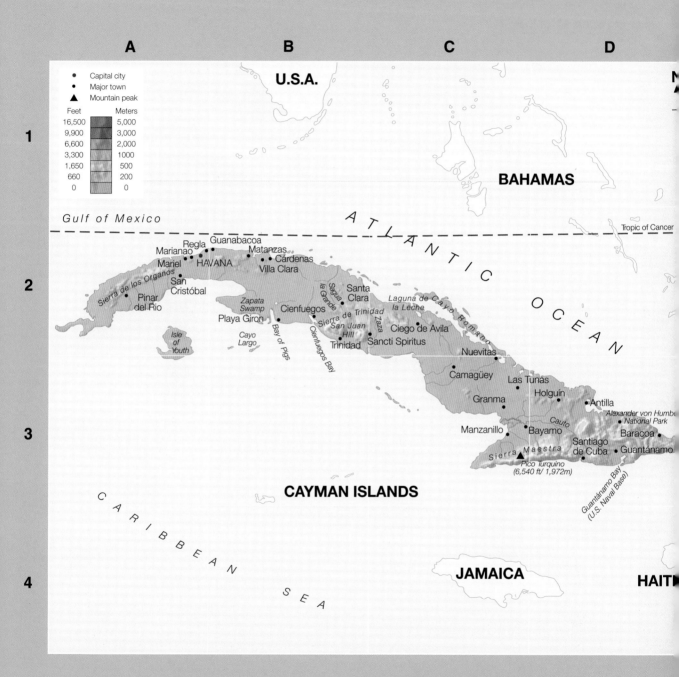

MAP OF CUBA

Alexander von Humboldt Natio-nal Park, D3
Antilla, D3
Atlantic Ocean, B1—B2, C1—C2, D2

Bahamas, C1—C2, D1
Baracoa, D3
Bay of Pigs, B2
Bayamo, C3

Camagüey, C3
Cárdenas, B2
Caribbean Sea, A3—A4, B3, C3
Cauto River, C3, D3
Cayman Islands, B3
Cayo Largo, B2
Cayo Romano, C2
Ciego de Avila, C2
Cienfuegos, B2
Cienfuegos Bay, B2

Granma, C3
Guanabacoa, B2
Guantánamo, D3
Guantánamo Bay, D3—D4
Gulf of Mexico, A2

Haiti, D4
Havana, A2
Holguín, D3

Isle of Youth, A2—A3

Jamaica, C4, D4

Laguna de la Leche, C2
Las Tunas, C3

Manzanillo, C3
Marianao, A2
Mariel, A2
Matanzas, B2

Nuevitas, C3

Pico Turquino, C3

Pinar del Rio, A2
Playa Giron, B2

Regla, A2

Sagua la Grande River, B2
San Cristóbal, A2
San Juan Hill, B2
Sancti Spiritus, C2
Santa Clara, B2
Santiago de Cuba, D3
Sierra de los Organos, A2

Sierra de Trinidad, B2
Sierra Maestra, C3, D3

Trinidad, B2
Tropic of Cancer, A2, B2, C2, D2

United States of America, B1

Villa Clara, B2

Zapata Swamp, B2
Zaza River, C2

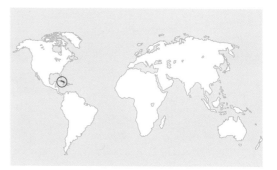

ECONOMIC CUBA

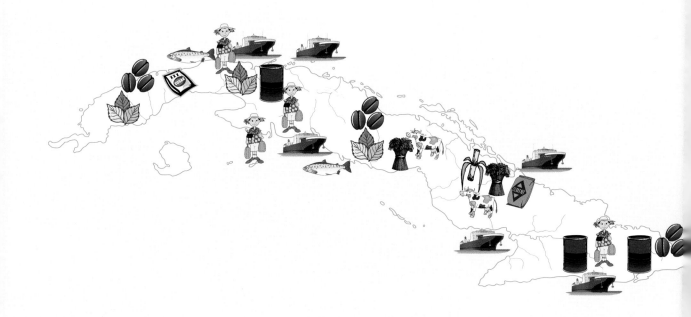

Farming

🐄 Cattle

🛢 Cement

Manufacturing

🛢 Oil Refinery

Sugar Mill

Services

🚢 Port

Tourism

Natural Resources

☕ Coffee

🐟 Fish

🌾 Rice

🌿 Sugar

🍃 Tobacco

ABOUT THE ECONOMY

OVERVIEW

The government is slowly reforming its socialist economic system while maintaining firm political control. At the 2011 Cuban Communist Party Congress, leaders approved a plan for wide-ranging economic changes. Nevertheless, the average Cuban's standard of living remains at a lower level than before the collapse of the Soviet Union.

GDP

$72.3 billion (2012)

GDP COMPOSITION BY SECTOR

Agriculture 3.9 percent; industry 22.3 percent; services 73.7 percent (2014)

INFLATION RATE

5.3 percent (2014)

CURRENCY

1 Cuba peso (CUP) = 100 centavos
Notes: 1, 3, 5, 10, 20, 50, 100, 200 pesos
Coins: 20 centavos; 1 and 3 pesos
USD 1 = CUP 26.5 (May 2015)

LAND AREA

42,792 square miles (110,860 square km)

LAND USE

Arable land, 30.8 percent; permanent crops, 3.5 percent, other 66.4 percent (2012)

NATURAL RESOURCES

Cobalt, nickel, iron ore, chromium, copper, salt, timber, silica, petroleum, arable land

INDUSTRIES

Petroleum, nickel, cobalt, pharmaceuticals, tobacco, construction, steel, cement, agricultural machinery, sugar

AGRICULTURE PRODUCTS

Sugar, tobacco, citrus, coffee, rice, potatoes, beans; livestock

EXPORTS

$5.6 billion (2014)
Petroleum, nickel, medical products, sugar, tobacco, fish, citrus, coffee

IMPORTS

$14.9 billion (2014)
Petroleum, food, machinery and equipment, chemicals

TRADE PARTNERS

Canada 16 percent, China 15.2 percent, Venezuela 14.2 percent, Spain 7.5 percent, Netherlands 5.6 percent (2013)

LABOR FORCE

5.09 million (2014)
Agriculture 19.7 percent, industry 17.1 percent, services 63.2 percent (2011)

UNEMPLOYMENT RATE

3.6 percent (2014) (Note: this is an official rate; unofficial estimate is about double.)

CULTURAL CUBA

OLD HAVANA

Situated on the shores of Havana Bay, Old Havana contains a number of buildings that date back to the period of Spanish colonization. In 1982, UNESCO declared the area a World Heritage Site. Apart from Old Havana, the city of Havana also has a number of art galleries and museums, and it regularly stages theater and music performances.

NATIONAL THEATER FESTI

This event in Camagüey showcases plays and recognizes individuals an organizations that are major contrib theater. Awards are also given to the plays, actors and actresses, music, a The Theater Festival is held biennial an important cultural event in Cuba.

DESEMBARCO DEL GRANM NATIONAL PARK

The Desembarco del Granma Natio in Cabo Cruz is a World Heritage S its uplifted marine terraces. Visitors to view the spectacular limestone me terraces, which range from 1,181 fe (360 m) above sea level to 591 fee below. Cabo Cruz was also the lan of Granma, the yacht that carried C eighty-two others from Mexico in 19

PRESIDEO MODELO

Fidel Castro was one of the many people incarcerated in this prison on the Isle of Youth, Cuba's largest offshore island. The maximum-security prison was opened in 1931 and based on the plans for a similar prison in Joliet, Illinois, in the United States.

CIÉNAGA DE ZAPATA BIOSPHERE RESERVE

The Ciénaga de Zapata Biosphere Reserve covers 1.5 million acres (15,000 ha), and is Cuba's largest protected area. It contains the Zapata Swamp, which is the only known wild habitat of about three thousand Cuban crocodiles. These crocodiles are endangered, live in freshwater swamps, and are known for their aggressiveness.

VARADERO

The popular resort of Varadero is located near the city of Matanzas. Tourists come here to explore the caves and enjoy the beach and cays. Varadero's waters are suitable for scuba diving, snorkeling, deep-sea fishing, yachting, and other water sports.

ALEXANDER VON HUMBOLDT NATIONAL PARK

This national park is a World Herit Site that straddles the provinces of Guantánamo and Holguín. It is ric with indigenous flora and fauna. T park is named after Alexander von Humboldt, a German naturalist wh explored South America in the ear nineteenth century.

ABOUT THE CULTURE

OFFICIAL NAME
Conventional long form: Republic of Cuba.
Conventional short form: Cuba

CAPITAL
Havana

OTHER MAJOR CITIES
Santiago de Cuba, Camagüey, Holguín

GOVERNMENT
Communist state

NATIONAL FLAG
Five equal horizontal stripes of blue and white, with a red triangle containing a white five-pointed star on the left.

NATIONAL ANTHEM
La Bayamesa ("The Bayamo Song")

POPULATION
11,047,251 (2014)

POPULATION GROWTH RATE
—0.14 percent (2014)

LITERACY RATE
99.8 percent (2015)

LIFE EXPECTANCY
Total population: 78.22 years
Men: 75.92 years
Women: 80.65 years (2014)

ETHNIC GROUPS
White, 64.1 percent; mestizo, 26.6 percent; black, 9.3 percent (2012)

MAJOR RELIGIONS
Roman Catholicism, Santería

OFFICIAL LANGUAGE
Spanish

IMPORTANT ANNIVERSARIES
Liberation Day (January 1), Labor Day (May 1), Remembrance of the National Revolution (July 25—27), Day of Cuban Culture (October 10), *Granma* landing anniversary (December 2), Christmas Day (December 25)

LEADERS IN POLITICS
Fidel Castro—former president, leader of the Cuban Revolution
Raúl Castro—president (since 2008)
Miguel Diaz-Canel—first vice president (since 2013)

LEADERS IN THE ARTS
Alicia Alonso (ballet dancer), Raúl Martínez (artist), Manuel Mendive (artist), Alejo Carpentier (writer), José Lezama Lima (poet), Compay Segundo (musician)

TIMELINE

IN CUBA	IN THE WORLD
1000 BCE The Ciboney and Guanahatabey migrate from Central America to Cuba.	**753 BCE** Rome is founded.
	600 CE Height of Mayan civilization
	1000 The Chinese perfect gunpowder and begin to use it in warfare.
1200 CE The Taíno settle in Cuba.	
1492 Christopher Columbus claims Cuba for Spain.	**1530** Beginning of transatlantic slave trade organized by the Portuguese in Africa.
	1558–1603 Reign of Elizabeth I of England
	1620 Pilgrims sail the *Mayflower* to America.
1762 British occupation of Havana	
1763 Treaty of Paris returns Havana to Spain.	**1776** US Declaration of Independence
	1789–1799 French Revolution
1895–1898 José Martí leads war of independence.	
1898 United States defeats Spain, wins control of Cuba.	
1902 Cuba becomes independent but remains under US protection.	
	1914–1918 World War I
1940 Fulgencio Batista elected president.	**1939–1945** World War II
	1949 The North Atlantic Treaty Organization (NATO) is formed.
1952 Batista seizes power for second time.	
1953 Fidel Castro leads an unsuccessful revolt.	

IN CUBA	IN THE WORLD
1956	
Castro returns to Cuba on *Granma*.	**1957**
1959	The Russians launch *Sputnik I.*
Castro leads a guerrilla army into Havana.	
1960	
Cuba nationalizes all US businesses. The United States places Cuba under embargo.	
1961	
Bay of Pigs invasion	
1962	
Cuban missile crisis	**1966–1969**
1976	The Chinese Cultural Revolution
Fidel Castro elected Cuban president	
1980	
Mariel boatlift	**1986**
	Nuclear power disaster at Chernobyl in Ukraine
1991	**1991**
Soviet military advisers leave Cuba.	Breakup of the Soviet Union
1996	
Helms-Burton Act tightens US embargo.	**1997**
1998	Hong Kong is returned to China.
Pope John Paul II visits Cuba.	
1999	
Elian Gonzalez found drifting off Florida coast. Both Cuba and United States claim him.	**2001**
	Terrorists crash planes in New York, Washington, DC, and Pennsylvania.
2008	**2008**
Fidel Castro steps down. Raúl Castro takes over.	United States elects first black president, Barack Obama.
2011	
Cuban law allows people to buy and sell private property for first time in fifty years.	**2014**
2015	Islamic State (ISIS) militant group proclaims worldwide caliphate. Takes control of large portions of the Middle East.
President Castro and President Barack Obama take steps to normalize relations.	
2015	**2015**
United States removes Cuba from state-sponsored terrorism list.	Pope Francis visits United States and Cuba in September.

GLOSSARY

cervecerías (sayr-vay-sayr-REE-as)
The equivalent of a bar or pub in Cuba.

Cold War
A state of political hostility between countries characterized by threats, propaganda, and sanctions, but no open warfare.

contradanza (kohn-tra-DAN-sa)
A traditional French country dance introduced to Cuba from Haiti.

counter-revolutionary
Someone who opposes and fights against the goals of a revolution.

criollos (kree-OH-yohs)
Cuban-born Spanish person; Creoles.

cult of personality
A system in which a leader is able to control a group of people through the sheer force of his or her personality and is often portrayed as a god-like figure.

danzón (dan-SOHN)
A Cuban dance related to the cha-cha.

El Tiempo Especial (el tee-EM-po es-spes-EE-ahl)
The Special Period, the Cuban economic crisis that followed the Soviet collapse.

Granma
The yacht that carried Fidel Castro, Che Guevara, and their followers to eastern Cuba in 1956, to overthrow the Batista government.

The name *Granma* was adopted as the name of the state-run newspaper.

machismo
An attitude and a form of behavior that assumes male dominance.

orisha (or-ISH-ah)
God or goddess in the Santería religion.

peninsulares (pay-nin-SOO-lah-rehs)
Spanish-born people living in Cuba.

Santería
Main Afro-Cuban religion practiced in Cuba.

socialismo o muerte (soh-see-ial-EES-mo oh moo-AIR-teh)
Literally "socialism or death," a Cuban political slogan.

son (son)
Indigenous music of Cuba.

Taíno
Early Native inhabitants of Cuba

tin-pot dictator
An autocratic ruler with little political credibility but with delusions of grandeur.

FOR FURTHER INFORMATION

BOOKS

Alonzo, Cynthia Carris. *Passage to Cuba: An Up-Close Look at the World's Most Colorful Culture*. New York: Skyhorse Publishing, 2015.

Castro, Fidel. *Che: A Memoir*. North Melbourne, Victoria, Australia: Ocean Press, 2006.

Cooke, Julia. *The Other Side of Paradise, Life in the New Cuba*. Berkley, CA: Seal Press/Perseus Books, 2014.

Frank, Marc. *Cuban Revelations, Behind the Scenes in Havana*. Gainsville, FL: University Press of Florida, 2015.

Garcia, Cristina. *Dreaming in Cuban*. New York: Random House, 1992.

Gjelten, Tom. *Bacardi and the Long Fight for Cuba: The Biography of a Cause*. New York: Penguin Books, 2009.

Hayden, Tom. *Listen, Yankee: Why Cuba Matters*. New York: Seven Stories Press, 2015.

Ramonet, Ignacio, and Fidel Castro. *Fidel Castro: My Life: A Spoken Autobiography*. New York: Scribner, 2006.

DVDS/FILMS

American Experience: Fidel Castro. PBS, 2005. DVD

Buena Vista Social Club. Artisan Entertainment, 2001. DVD

Cuba Feliz. Lorber, 2004.

Cuba: The Accidental Eden. PBS, 2010. DVD.

Strawberry and Chocolate. Buena Vista Home Video, 1995.

MUSIC

A Toda Cuba le Gusta. Nonesuch, 1997.

Buena Vista Social Club. Nonesuch, 1997.

Cafe Cubano. Putumayo World Music, 2008.

The Rough Guide to Cuban Son. World Music Network, 2000.

WEBSITES

BBC News, Cuba profile — Timeline, www.bbc.com/news/world-latin-america-19576144

CIA World Factbook, www.cia.gov/library/publications/the-world-factbook/geos/cu.html

Cuba Absolutely, www.cubaabsolutely.com

Lonely Planet, Cuba www.lonelyplanet.com/cuba

Taste of Cuba.com, www.tasteofcuba.com

The New York Times Topics, Cuba, topics.nytimes.com/top/news/international/countriesandterritories/cuba/index.html

BIBLIOGRAPHY

WEBSITES

BBC News, Cuba profile — Timeline, www.bbc.com/news/world-latin-america-19576144

CIA World Factbook, www.cia.gov/library/publications/the-world-factbook/geos/cu.html

Council on Foreign Relations, www.cfr.org/cuba/us-cuba-relations/p11113

Cuba Absolutely, www.cubaabsolutely.com

Cuba Ministry of Foreign Affairs, www.cubaminrex.cu/en

Cuba Naturaleza, www.cubanaturaleza.org/en

Encyclopedia of Earth, Cuba, www.eoearth.org/view/article/151558

Environmental Defense Fund, "Securing a Sustainable Future for Cuba's Fisheries,"
    www.edf.org/oceans/cuba-crossroads

GlobalSecurity.org, www.globalsecurity.org/military/world/cuba/economy.htm

Lamrani, Salim, "Cuba's Health Care System: a Model for the World," *Huffington Post*,
    www.huffingtonpost.com/salim-lamrani/cubas-health-care-system-_b_5649968.html

McClatchy Newspapers, "New attitudes on once-taboo race questions emerge in Cuba," Pop
    Matters, June 25, 2007. www.popmatters.com/article/new-attitudes-on-once-taboo-race-
    questions-emerge-in-cuba

Migration Policy Institute, www.migrationpolicy.org/article/cuban-immigrants-united-states

Moffett, Dan, "U.S. Allows Cuban Migrants Different Treatment," About.com, immigration.about.
    com/od/immigrationlawandpolicy/a/U-S-Allows-Cuban-Migrants-Different-Treatment.htm

NPR, "Scientists Work to Protect Cuba's Unspoiled Reefs," www.npr.org/templates/story/story.
    php?storyId=121177851

Pew Research Center, www.pewresearch.org/fact-tank/2014/12/23/as-cuban-american-
    demographics-change-so-do-views-of-cuba

Reporters Without Borders, "Details About Cuba," index.rsf.org/#!/index-details/CUB
    ———. "Internet Enemies, Cuba" en.rsf.org/internet-enemie-cuba,39756.html

Santeria Church of the Orishas, santeriachurch.org

Siegelbaum, Portia, "Cuba Economic Reforms Felt at the Dinner Table," CBS News, Dec. 31,
    2013, www.cbsnews.com/news/cuba-economic-reforms-felt-at-the-dinner-table

Silva, Christina, "Why Cubans Are Still Risking Their Lives On Flimsy Rafts To Leave The Island,"
    International Business Times, May 7, 2015, www.ibtimes.com/why-cubans-are-still-risking-
    their-lives-flimsy-rafts-leave-island-1909877

Taste of Cuba.com, www.tasteofcuba.com

The *New York Times* Topics, Cuba, topics.nytimes.com/top/news/international/
    countriesandterritories/cuba/index.html

US Naval Station Guantanamo Bay, www.cnic.navy.mil/regions/cnrse/installations/ns_
    guantanamo_bay.html

World Atlas, www.worldatlas.com/webimage/countrys/namerica/caribb/cuba/culand.htm

INDEX

INDEX